WELSH MOD
our story

'True it's a dream mixed with nostalgia'

PAUL WELLER
Tales From The Riverbank

DEDICATED TO THE MEMORY
OF A LIFE-LONG MODERNIST

HUGH LLOYD
13th September 1949 – 5th January 2017

"I first got into mod about 1965. In the 60s, Caerphilly and Cardiff were the places to hear and see mod music. We used to frequent a place called the Boars Head in Caerphilly for a night called The Caerphilly Disc. They would play Motown, Spencer Davis and that kind of thing. It was 50p to get in and we went every Saturday.

"We would also go to see bands in the Pavilion in Porthcawl. The one I'll always remember was the Stax show at The Top Rank in Cardiff. It was something else! Top of the bill was Otis Redding. He wore a proper mod suit and I was in the front. I've never forgotten it.

"I used to buy my suits from Burtons in Cardiff. A mohair suit was a must – three buttons, two pockets on one side. My thing was a full length leather coat, which would cost about £20 in those days. You would get a ticket from Burtons and pay for it each week."

"It was just a marvellous time."

INTRODUCTION

Mod in Wales: clean living under different circumstances

When most people think of mod they think of Soho, Carnaby Street, Brighton and Margate. And who can blame them? London was the epicentre of Mod and its nucleus was Soho. Here, in late 50s, a small group of hip London lads started making distinct style choices that differentiated them from their peers.

They opted for a more European cut to their clothes and, when it came to music, their taste was mainly American and black, eschewing 'trad' jazz and white rock and roll for modern jazz and Bebop. They were tired of dowdy post-war Britain and its associated values. They thought, as in the title of Miles Davis' 1957 album – they were the 'Birth of Cool.'

"*Mod is the closest the British have come to constructing their own version of the American Dream,*" writes Richard Weight in *Mod: A Very British Style* – and he is spot on.

Young people in Britain were used to being defined by their class and their parents expectations. Now with more freedom and disposable income they could define themselves - and they did so with clothes and music.

Many claim that mod in its purest form was over by 1962. But Mod evolved. Its style became more commercial, its music more common-place and its reach geographically much wider. Mod spread to 'the provinces' and as this book aims to show, gained a particular foothold in South Wales and the Valleys.

Wales in the 60s was still heavily industrialised, the chapel-going way of life was still dominant. But changes brought about through immigration during the turn of the century saw new communities moving here for work – in particular, the Italians, who opened cafés and ice-cream parlours that introduced the Welsh to some of the delights of continental living.

The unique mix of close-knit, terraced communities that lined the Welsh hills and filled its valleys were natural breeding grounds for allegiances and rivalries among its youth. So when the mod subculture edged its way west from London, it acted like a magnet for those looking for something more stylish than the 50s hangover that was the 'rocker,' or more locally referred to as 'the greaser'.

> "Mod is more than just a memory for these people. It's a feeling that can be re-ignited readily should a needle hit the groove on the right piece of vinyl"

These communities weren't wealthy, so anything you could do to mark yourself out as different was very attractive to those who wanted 'to be someone.' As early as 1962 there are tales of small pockets of mods wearing John Smedley knitwear and Chelsea boots, hanging around street corners with their transistor radios, listening the the likes of The Kinks or The Who.

Often there would only be a handful of them. Certain streets were mod, depending who lived there, others were home to rockers. They would do their best most of the time to avoid each other. But pitched battles were common and, much like in the south coast seaside towns of Brighton and Margate, Welsh mods would make their own Bank Holiday pilgrimage to the South Wales resorts of Porthcawl and Barry Island and Rhyl and Llandudno in the north.

In this book we have been privileged to speak to and photograph several original mods from Wales, who have been glad to share their memories of being a mod during that transformative era – be it, saving up for their first suit, hearing Motown for the first time, or the rush of seeing heads turn while riding their newly purchased Lambretta.

We have also tracked down 60s mod group, The Eyes of Blue from Neath, whose legions of Welsh fans, dressed in their mod finery would follow them around the country to gigs supporting the likes of Georgie Fame, The Who and The Animals. When the London bands turned up to play at the Ritz in Neath, they were surprised to see their local support act better kitted out in the latest mod gear than they were.

Someone who was around during the very inception of the mod movement in the late 50s was Ebbw Vale-born fashion designer Jeff Banks. Along with his fashion contemporaries, Jeff helped direct the 'youth-quake' that took place in the 60s, by introducing young British designers such as Foale & Tuffin and Moya Bowler to hip customers through his Blackheath store, Clobber.

In this book he gives us a fabulously detailed glimpse of the almost obsessional attention to detail that was the raison d'etre of the early London mods, who were the blueprint for everything that followed.

Our Welsh Mod journey then takes us on into the skinhead era of the late 60s and early 70s and how the style tribes took to the terraces to frame their allegiances. We then move into the punk and new wave era and mod's re-incarnation in the late 70s into what is now known as 'the revival' which was given a further shot in the arm with the release of the cult film *Quadrophenia*.

Much like in the 60s, the mod revival burnt itself out as soon as it became a media plaything and in the mid-80s there was a distinct split between those in search of more authentic style and music cues and those who were happy to live it up as part of the scooter scene. Scooterists enjoyed the many organised rallies, including our own Welsh national rallies now held alternately in Tenby and Llandudno.

Those who hung onto mod, tended to go back underground – heading up to London in search of smart suits and 60s RnB. Then when Britpop exploded, a new generation took up the baton with a nod to their elder style statesmen, Paul Weller, who was once again riding high in the charts. Those that still carried a torch for mod were once again vindicated.

As the 90s moved into a new millennium, mod spun into new musical and style directions – many sought out newer and rarer grooves on the fringes of the dance scene. Northern Soul was again revived as a younger generation began to enjoy the delights of sliding and spinning across a talc-dusted dance floor. Northern Soul is still huge in North Wales, a tradition born of its close proximity to the soul meccas of Wigan and Blackpool.

Today, even the young have become nostalgic for a period in time that only their parents or grandparents knew about. The retro and vintage obsession of the last few years has in turn brought a more youthful element to the mod fold – who are happy to take something old and something new and move it forward.

As well as providing a kind of mod timeline across Wales, this book will, I hope, also act as a cultural document of people, places and memories that might otherwise not have been saved or shared. There are some people featured in this book that are no longer with us, there are those that in the twilight of their life have felt re-energised once they have realised that there are people fascinated by the clothes and music of their youth.

Mod is more than just a memory for these people. It's a feeling that can be re-ignited readily should a needle hit the groove on the right piece of vinyl. And from the conversations shared over the course of the last 18 months of this book project, it has become clear that 50 years feels like the blink of an eye for those who count themselves lucky enough to have been influenced by what has become Britain's most enduring subculture.

— Claire Mahoney

CONTENTS

CHAPTER ONE   **I'm not like everybody else**

- 18   Alan Wells
- 22   Jeff Banks
- 26   Geoff Nicholas
- 28   Andy Fairweather Low
- 34   Terence Evans
- 36   Cob Records
- 38   Wyndham Rees
- 44   Paul Matthews
- 48   Café Society

CHAPTER TWO   **Days of change**

- 54   Bryn Gregory
- 58   Chris Jones
- 60   Andrew and Mike Knowles
- 62   Lewgi Lewis
- 64   Evan Wyn Davis
- 68   Eddie Crole
- 72   Fanzines

CHAPTER THREE   **Saturday's kids**

- 78   Steve Garland
- 84   Carl Grisley
- 86   Paul 'Sammy' Thomas
- 90   Darren and June Luker
- 92   Mike Caluan
- 96   Jane Williams

CHAPTER FOUR   **Shadows and reflections**

- 102   Jonny Owen
- 106   Peter Jachimiak
- 110   Des Mannay

CHAPTER FIVE   **Dedicated followers of fashion**

- 116   Paul Mansfield
- 120   James Parker
- 124   Adam Lewis
- 128   Simon Quinn
- 132   Phil Matsell
- 136   Lesley Herbert
- 138   Gillian Finney-Richards
- 140   Abigail Rachel

CHAPTER ONE

I'm not like everybody else

60s originals and movers and shakers

"Before mod everything seemed boring, old fashioned and lacking in style"

ALAN WELLS
Original mod and still going strong, Rhydyfelin

"It was 1963, and we were 16. My best mate Bernard Crockett and I were staying in Catford, south London with Bernard's aunt and uncle. We decided to go into the 'smoke,' the colloquial term at that time for inner London.

"I'm sitting in Lord John's, Carnaby Street trying a pair of shoes on. A guy sits next to me and starts to put on the same shoes. Still with my head down I say, *'great choice'* and look up to see Mick Jagger. For me it was the start of my mod journey.

"I was brought up in a terraced council house in Rhydyfelin by my grandparents. They couldn't afford a television which, for me, turned out well. They owned an old radiogram cabinet on which I tuned into Radio Luxembourg and initially discovered Chuck Berry, Little Richard and Rhythm & Blues.

"Before mod everything seemed boring, old-fashioned and lacking in style. As mods we thought we were smarter in clothes, outlook, ambition and intelligence and our girlfriends, many of whom became our wives, were the same.

"We wanted to improve ourselves for the better things in life. We wanted top jobs with top pay and were willing to try harder to achieve this. We thought that rockers were old-fashioned, backward-looking and dirty. They thought we were posers, dressed too smartly and were effeminate.

"This friction led to many weekend 'set toos' at the local dance halls and discotheques. Not many Friday nights in 1964 went by without a fracas of some sort. At that time mods were seriously outnumbered by the rockers who carried flick knives and knuckledusters. There were some serious beatings on many weekends and I'm sad to say, we learnt to run fast.

"These conflicts continued in Barry and Porthcawl and not just on Bank Holidays. Mods and rockers would converge from all over South Wales. In 1963/1964, as in

> "My pockets were never unstitched so that the cut, look and fall of the jacket always looked just right, sharp. The pocket handkerchief matched the tie, if you were wearing one. Shoes always matched the belt colour and tone"

Pontypridd, we were outnumbered, but by 1965/1966 we were in the ascendancy and revenge was sweet.

"My suits were all made to measure by Sid Hoffman tailors of Sardis Road, Pontypridd and always to my designs. Mohair mostly and of varying colours. Blue, a dark burgundy, beige, dark green are some I recall, together with a light grey herringbone. My suits varied between side and centre vents, but all vents were deep. One centre vent started at my shoulder blades.

"In 1964/1965 suits always had ticket pockets, narrow lapels, and a mod must – the pocket handkerchief. My pockets were never unstitched so that the cut, look and fall of the jacket always looked just right, sharp. The pocket handkerchief matched the tie, if you were wearing one. Shoes always matched the belt colour and tone.

"My raincoats and overcoats were also made to my designs and always included a ticket pocket and pocket handkerchief which matched the handkerchief of the suit. Most of my closest friends as mods designed their own clothes. This gave them a uniqueness and difference which kept them at the forefront of mod.

"So here I am at 70, jogging along, as the youngsters might say. Following trends now, not setting them but still keeping in my heart the desire to look good. The early sounds of Atlantic, Stax, Motown and Bluebeat still move me. It's in my soul."

I'm not like everybody else Alan Wells

"Pete Townsend once said to me that if you were a mod you always carried your rain coat over your right arm and not over your left arm – because that is what your dad did"

JEFF BANKS
Fashion designer & TV presenter, Ebbw Vale & London

"I started having my clothes made to measure when I was 15 or 16. I was specific about the kind of suits and shirts that I wore. Winkle-picker shoes with a Cuban heel were *de-rigueur* – Denson's made them. But if you really wanted to elevate your stature there was a guy in Battersea called Stan who made shoes and if you were a serious modernist that's where you would go. You would also wear collarless shirts with a stiff white collar and we would all take them to specific launderies to have them starched and polished.

"On your scooter you would wear a straw Sinatra hat and always a Raglan sleeve beige raincoat. On Saturday lunchtime you would probably wear a Gabicci shirt with panelling on it and very narrow trousers with a raincoat. But on Friday, Saturday night and Sunday lunchtime you always wore a stiff collar. The collars had to be absolutely immaculate. They would only be worn once before they were re-laundered. So when I went out on Friday night I always carried a box of spare collars with me on the back of my scooter. So if I pulled a bird on Friday night and was going down the pub on a Saturday lunchtime or straight out on Saturday night – I had a smart white collar. That was the spirit of the era and everyone was very particular about the finesse of your clothing – be it the combination of ties and shirts, the pocket hanker-chiefs.

"There was a very specific cut to the suit. The shoulders were quite soft and the waist was actually cut slightly higher to exaggerate a kind of high waist and the lapels were narrow. Even though the suit was boxed Italian, it had a kind of North American Ivy League

connotation about it. You would go into detail about how wide the pocket flaps were and whether or not you would have an extra ticket pocket on the outside. So all of this was noticed by your friends when you actually rolled up in your latest creation. It could be three-button, two-button, single-button, but very rarely double breasted. I wore the occasional cotton double-breasted blazer, but very rarely a tailored double-breasted suit.

"We opened Clobber in Blackheath in 1964. Clobber stocked mainly women's wear. We stocked brands like Foal & Tuffin, Sam 90 and Janice Ainwright. They were all ex-Royal College of Art students who were making very modern and contemporary fashion. We also stocked a great shoe designer called Moya Bowler who did the ultimate mod shoes for that era.

"The block is the fundamental pattern. So when you are creating a suit look, you start off with your block pattern, which determines how big the shoulder pads are going to be, how wide the shoulders are and where the waist is going to be. It's the fundamental foundation – the building brick.

"I normally have three blocks running at any one time. I have my classic block, which is a middle-aged man block, I have my tailored block for the young man who wants a straight shoulder and a nipped-in waist – very much a Saville Row look and then I have my Ivy League block, which has got virtually no shoulder pads in it with a slightly boxier jacket. That is our mod look. And I vary them from that. Every year I tweak and mess about. There is always a new take on it. My current Jeff Banks Brit collection is pure mod and aimed at 17-20-year-old prom customers.

> "We came out the Second World War into a ration book era. So the mod movement that kicked off around 1958/1959 was a two fingers up to the establishment. It meant you didn't have to cut the Mars Bar into seven slices and have a little bit of it every day"

"I wouldn't do now exactly what I was doing in the 1960s. Technology has changed, the sewing capability with modern machinery has changed. We used to wear mohair suits in the 60s with a real sheen to them – that Tony Bennet/Sammy Davis Jr look. I wouldn't do them as shiny as that anymore because the fabric is much lighter these days. In those days we would be using a fabric that weighed 11oz a yard and now it is 8oz a square metre. So it is much lighter and more delicate.

"Pete Townsend once said to me that if you were a mod you always carried your rain coat over your right arm and not over your left arm – because that is what your dad did. He said he can remember going into a bank for an interview and he had his raincoat over his right arm. He said he could see the bank manager looking at him and thinking: *There is something odd about this guy. He is smart, he's tidy, he's got a hair-cut – but there is something rebellious about him*. It was the raincoat.

"We came out the Second World War into a ration book era and the mod movement that kicked off around 1958/1959 was a two fingers up to the establishment. It meant you didn't have to cut the Mars Bar into seven slices and have a little bit of it every day. You didn't have to make do with two ounces of sugar a week, you could actually go the whole hog and be who you are and what you are, regardless of where you came from.

"It didn't matter if you came from somewhere like Ebbw Vale. It was a revolutionary point in the whole make-up of society. London was the epicentre of it – there was no fashion anywhere else. It all happened here and that shockwave changed the world and made you believe you could be whoever you wanted to be."

I'm not like everybody else Jeff Banks

"Songwriters of the day were our age and put into song lyrics exactly what we were feeling"

GEOFF NICHOLAS
Original 60s mod, Gwent

"The 50s and 60s youth were starved of their own music. The only daytime radio station with music was the BBC Light Programme. It was Radio Luxembourg that gave us 'pop' music, and this station only broadcast after 7:00pm with a very poor signal. It's no wonder that many turned to making their own music and improvising. So with the family transistor radio under my pillow at night, (like so many others), I could listen to the music of my generation fading in and out.

"1960 saw me turn 13. An important time in anyone's life. A time when I discovered dances and girls. The music of rock and roll was interesting, but this had echoes of teddy boys, and they were not the image I saw myself in. In north Gwent nothing went on past 10pm because of fights and if you were still there at ten-past-ten, you were lucky.

"Between 1961-1963 things started to change for me with The Beatles coming along and the Mersey Sound. The haircut was the first thing to change. My hair at the time was a crew cut, but it soon was grown into a 'Beatle' cut. For me their first album *Please Please Me* was the best ever.

"It's hard to describe what it is like to hear some of these sounds for the first time when you are 15 and have never heard them before. Songwriters of the day were our age and put into song lyrics exactly what we were feeling. The pains of youth expressed through the medium of music that we danced to. Waiting for the music chart show on a Sunday night was the highlight of the week. New music every week.

"I got my first scooter when I was 19. The scooter had no wing mirrors simply because I couldn't afford them. It was lucky that I could afford the crash bars and the screen. After the scooter I had a Mini.

"Mine was rather special. It was a green and black 850, which I customised by ripping out the dashboard and putting my own in. I then bought a new Mini van that had been in a crash for £75. The engine was perfect, so I stuck it in my Mini. My girlfriend also had a Mini and the engine later went into her car. So it went into three different vehicles over time."

I'm not like everybody else

"It didn't matter where you played – you were always billed as direct from London, never direct from Wales"

ANDY FAIRWEATHER LOW
Guitarist, songwriter & producer, Cardiff

Cardiff group Amen Corner were named after a weekly club night in the Victoria Ballroom in the Canton part of the city, where on Sundays DJ Dr Rock would spin all the latest soul tunes from America.

The band were initially a soul and blues outfit, but like many bands at the time, once they signed to a major label, they found themselves steered in a much more commerical direction. Their first hit single was *Gin House* which went into the charts in 1967, while the band were on the Deram label. The following year they reached number three with *Bend Me, Shape Me*. They were the first Welsh group to reach the Number 1 spot in the charts after moving from Deram to Andrew Loog Oldham's Immediate label. The year was 1969 and the song, *(If Paradise is) Half as Nice*.

The band disbanded at the end of 1969 after recording their swansong album, *Farewell to the Real Magnificent Seven*. Andy and band members Clive Taylor, Dennis Bryon, Blue Weaver and Neil Jones re-grouped under the name Fairweather, scoring a UK Number 6 hit with *Natural Sinner*. The band disbanded soon after and Andy went onto to have a successful solo career playing with Eric Clapton, George Harrison and Roger Waters.

"I used to 'mitch' off school to go to Barretts music shop in Cardiff. Dave Edmunds worked there and there would always be loads of bands coming in and these fantastic guitars hanging up on the wall. Then when I started working myself there I got to spend all my time there which was great.

"There were lots of mods around, certainly in the cafés around Cardiff. The style, the mohair suits, button-down shirts, the smell of Brut aftershave – that's a real strong memory for me to this day. I always had a love of black American music. In fact, that's how I started. We were playing these clubs in Cardiff and they would

Opposite page: Amen Corner in 1968

© Pictorial Press Ltd / Alamy

have these fantastic sound systems with these great big Seeburg speakers with black American soul music coming out of them.

"A lot of this music would come up through the clubs in Cardiff Bay. Early Booker T, Otis Redding, all the Stax stuff. Which is exactly what Amen Corner eventually grew into being. But even before we formed Amen Corner, all we did was play Stax and Atlantic material.

"I remember one night in Swindon. *Knock on Wood* had just come out. We played it once and then we were asked to play it again. In the end we played it eight times!

"*Midnight Hour*, *Mr Pitiful*, you name it, it was all fantastic music which still stays with me and I still do a little soul revue in my show now. So nothing has really changed since that point on.

"We were one of the first Cardiff bands to play the Ritz in Skewen where local band Eyes of Blue has a residency. We were in a competition with them and I'll never forget it, because we lost and the reason we were beaten by the Eyes of Blue was because they were better. They looked better, they played better, they sang better. They were a fantastic band and fantastic bunch of musicians."

"We were both signed to Deram. It was a quite a hip label, I remember Procol Harum was on there. *Whiter Shade of Pale* was and is still one of my all time favourite songs. It didn't matter where you played – you were always billed as direct from London, never direct from Wales. All bands in that particular time had to come from London. We went to London in 1966 and in 1967 *Gin House* came out. If I had got to London in 1964, that would have been the period for me. All the bands I grew to love were around then -The Small Faces, The Who and The Kinks.

"Up until then we were taking songs written by other people. But with The Beatles everything changed. They just took it to another level. They made it the case that you could write your own songs, you could do it yourself and you didn't have to go to other writers.

"Ron King got us our first dates in Bournemouth and other venues that he used to run: Romford, Borehamwood, Barnet. He'd even hold a rehearsal and charge people to come in. He didn't rip us off at that stage. He took us on as a band and then ripped us off. He then handed us onto Small Faces manager, Don Arden, who also ripped us off. From there we went to Andrew Loog Oldham and the rest is history.

"The truth is it is all in the past, and if I had got any of that money, I probably wouldn't have done anything good with it. It was all about how far eventually I was going to fall, and I didn't fall very far when it all fell apart. I don't understand the music business today. I'm not really particularly fond of it. My money today is made by playing to people live. I know no more than that. When I brought out my album *Zone-O-Tone* and took it to the head of Radio 2, he said: *"Don't bother bringing me this album because I ain't gonna play it"*.

"Keep it in mind. I've had my 15 minutes. In fact, I have had my 15 minutes more than a few times. It's ok, we are out there playing. I've just finished playing tonight as it happens and people are coming up to me, and you know what? I love it now more than I ever did."

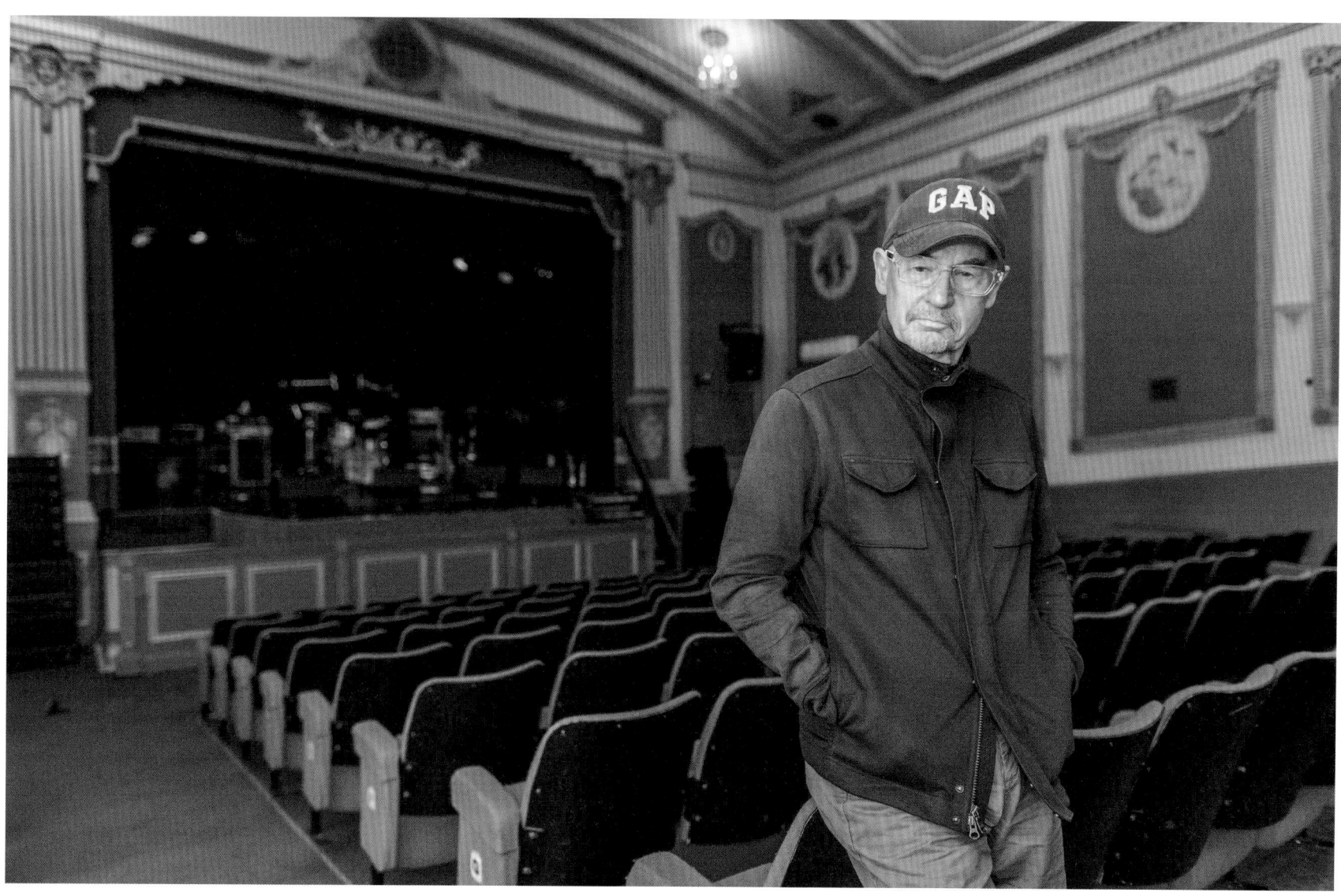

I'm not like everybody else Andy Fairweather Low

"I used to feel like a peacock in my suit on my scooter. The more mirrors you had, the better the bird you'd get on the back"

TERENCE EVANS
Original 60s mod and scooterist, Cardiff

"I left school at 15 and started working down Smith's Radiators on Tudor Lane in Ely, Cardiff. There was a guy there that had a scooter – a Lambretta. He was older than me but he used to take me on the back and we'd go down to places like Penarth. Where I lived, it was all Teddy Boys and rock & roll and I wasn't into that, so when The Rolling Stones and The Who came out, I starting listening to them. We would go into Spiller's Records on The Hayes in Cardiff and listen to the records in the booths or we'd go to the Sasaparilla bar in the arcade and ask them to play the records we liked.

"When I was 17 I decided that I wanted a scooter myself and so I asked my father. We used to go down to Bevan's shop opposite the castle and look at all the scooters on the weekend. I paid just over £100 for a Lambretta and had a Union Jack painted on the sides by a welder chap we knew that was also a good artist.

"My father was always smartly dressed. He was a welder, but he still used to always wear a suit and tie. He took me to Burton's in town to get my first suit. I got a three-piece suit with covered buttons which cost me about £8.

"There was also a tailor behind my mother's house. He was Italian as well. You would go into his home and it would be like a proper tailors with dummies with people's suits on that he was making. He would always have a long tape round his neck and a pair of scissors in his hand. I would take in pictures from magazines and say '*I want something like that*', and it would never be a problem.

"I used to feel like a peacock in my suit on my scooter. The more mirrors you had, the better the bird you'd get on the back. About 15 years ago I got back into scootering and bought a GTS. I've got two GTS's now, but one has got a side car. My father had a side-car with his motorbike that I always used to sit in. I took my side-car to the Isle of Wight rally one year and had to go at the front of the ride-out. So there I was with about 16,000 scooters behind me without a clue where I was going!"

"At its height in 1971 Cob was sending out over 7,500 records a week to some 25,000 customers in over 50 countries around the world"

COB RECORDS
Porthmadog

The legendary Cob Records began life in Porthmadog in 1967 in a back room of the family-run café on the same site opposite the railway station where the vintage steam trains still alight to this day.

In the 60s, the café was the perfect hang-out for local mods. But there was no record shop in the area. So founder Brian Davies asked his parents, who ran the café, whether they would let him sell ex-juke-box singles in a space in the basement. Business took off straight away.

Demand soon outstripped supply so Davies persuaded the rest of the family that they open accounts with the major record labels and let the record shop take over the whole basement of the café. The shop did so well that it soon moved upstairs and the original café business gave way to the record business that is still going strong today.

The shop prides itself on its extensive second-hand collection of vinyl and CDs. The collection grew from the original swap-and-sell idea. LPs retailing at 32/6d were still quite pricey for most people – so Cob offered its customers the option to trade three of their own old LPs for any new one.

At its height in 1971 Cob was sending out over 7,500 records a week to some 25,000 customers in over 50 countries around the world. It also opened a second store in Bangor which is sadly now closed. Famous customers include Robert Plant, Jools Holland, Ian Brown, Sir Antony Hopkins, Billy Bragg and Mike Peters of the Alarm. Cob also did a lot of business with the late radio DJ John Peel.

The majority of the shop's business still comes from second-hand sales, with particular demand for 60s,70s and 80s music. Holiday-makers, who pay an annual visit to the store, usually leave with bags full of records - having visiting the shop over many years each summer. Now, of course, the majority of the mail-order side of the business is done online.

Cob has over 9,000 second-hand CDs and rarities and if there is something you can't find – Cob can probably find it for you.

I'm not like everbody else

"We used to drive through the night to Sheffield after a gig at the Ritz in Skewen, wash in the council toilets in the morning and then play King Mojo on the Sunday and then drive back and go to work Monday"

WYNDHAM REES
Singer, Eyes of Blue and Faded Glory, Neath

The Eyes of Blue were a soul and RnB band based in Neath, who became very popular on the South Wales gig circuit in the 60s. They were the regular support band at The Ritz in Skewen where they were billed before the likes of Chris Farlowe, The Who and The Animals.

In 1966 they took part in the *Melody Maker* Beat contest. The prize was a year's recording contract with Decca and £1000 worth of music equipment. Over 12 coaches from South Wales followed the band down to the finals at the London Palladium. They won, beating their Welsh rivals, Amen Corner. That same year they went on a 16-date tour for Radio London with Georgie Fame.

Their single *Supermarket Full of Cans* released on the Decca subsidiary, Deram has since become a regular fixture on Northern Soul playlists. They also recorded their own sterling version of The Parliaments' *Heart Trouble*.

When the Decca contract finished, they were picked up by Mercury Records where they cut their first album at Chappell Studios in London. The album: *Crossroads of Time* was released in the spring of 1969 and marked the band's passage into the psych era. The sleeve notes and two of the songs on the album, including the title track, *Crossroads of Time* and *Love is the Law*, were written by Graham Bond. After three albums 'The Eyes' bowed out to a home crowd at Neath's Gwyn Hall – the same venue they had played their very first gig.

I'm not like everybody else

Opposite page: Ray 'Taff' Williams and Wyndham Rees

"Every weekend we would go shopping. We often bought mohair suits in Morris Cowan's in Swansea. Me and Taff also got other clothes from there"

"Late 1962/1963 was when 'The Eyes' as a four piece really started. Before that me and 'Taff' (Ray Williams) were in a group called The Mustangs. We did Eddie Cochran, Gene Vincent and Ricky Nelson stuff, all round the local pubs and clubs.

"When we won a recording contract with Decca we were put on the Deram label. Cat Stevens was the number one artist on it at the time and we were number two. Later that year we did the Georgie Fame tour. We opened at the Hammersmith Odeon and then toured all over the country in one tour bus with all the artists. There was Eric Burdon & The Animals, Chris Farlowe, The Paul Buttlerfield Blues Band and Geno Washington.

"When we were gigging in London we used to stay in a hotel called The Madison, which was near Paddington – all the bands used to stay there. We would play all the clubs, including The Speakeasy when Jonnie Walker was a DJ there.

"We also played Peter Stringfellow's King Mojo club in Sheffield once a month. We used to drive through the night to Sheffield after a gig at the Ritz in Skewen, wash in the council toilets in the morning and then play King Mojo on the Sunday and then drive back and go to work Monday.

"I was 22 when the band hit the big time. I was the only one that could drive to start with, so I took everyone around. We had a massive local mod following. When we did the London Palladium we had twelve 52-seater buses going up. They came from all over South Wales: Port Talbot, Swansea, Neath, Llanelli, Ammanford. Many of the girls on board had thumbed a lift with us.

"At Deram we weren't allowed to do our own songs. We had a producer called Noel Walker and he was very strict. Him and his team wrote *Supermarket Full of Cans* and therefore they got the royalties. We then went to Mercury where we released *Crossroads of Time* with Graham Bond who wrote a lot of the songs on there. I remember supporting The Graham Bond Organisation one time and they were absolutely out of it. We had to take them to a bent chemists on the Sunday morning to get some more drugs as they were so wasted.

"Every weekend we would go shopping. We often bought mohair suits in Morris Cowan's in Swansea. We ordered them and had them fitted to size. Me and Taff also got other clothes from there. I had a full-length,

I'm not like everybody else Wyndham Rees

Opposite page: The Eyes of Blue winning the Melody Maker National Beat Contest in 1966

© Pictorial Press Ltd / Alamy

belted red leather coat and he had a full-length, belted, beige suede one with shoes to match. Of course, when we got famous instead of buying shoes in Swansea we were getting them from Toppers in Carnaby Street.

"We would just walk around town looking like 'jack the lad' with all these girls following us around. They were all dressed up in the latest mod gear as well. I remember when we opened for The Who. I don't think they expected us to be dressed in the latest mod gear. So it was like: *"Follow that lovely boy!"*

"I had a friend who was a DJ, so I used to get all the American imports from him and that's how I copped onto all the early Tamla and soul stuff. That's how we changed from a mainly RnB set with The Mustangs and the early 'Eyes,' to a more soul sound.

"My voice was a bit higher than most. I was lead choir boy in St Catwgs Church in Neath. I would be in there three times on a Sunday in my cassock. I was lead choirist every Christmas. Obviously my voice dropped and I started listening and singing to music played on the Jack Jackson show on Radio Luxembourg.

"We had a massive following in Swansea too. We used to play at St Benedicts Church – or Bennys as it was known. Amen Corner used to play there as well. People would queue round the corner to get in and it would be packed – there were no fire regs in those days.

"Jayvee Entertainments, our promoters, put us forward for the *Melody Maker* competition. It was the only way to get us known outside of Wales. They wouldn't come past Cardiff because they thought we were all 'shunnies' and sheep farmers down here.

"We went down a storm everywhere especially in places like Brixton doing all the Tamla stuff. Temptations, Four Tops, Otis Reading, Wilson Pickett. We had six voices, four in the back and me and Gary in the front. Taff used to do all the harmonies, the 5ths, 7ths and the 9ths.

"We were dissapointed when Amen Corner had a hit with *Gin House Blues* – we were the kosher band of South Wales at the time, but we didn't hit the big time because the producer they gave us didn't want to do the stuff we were doing. We ended up with *Up and Down* and a *Supermarket Full of Cans*. It wasn't in our style at all. I wouldn't want to learn that song again, because it was something we were against and it wasn't our choice."

> "I remember when we opened for The Who. I don't think they expected us to be dressed in the latest mod gear. So it was like: *Follow that lovely boy!*"

"You were trying to be someone. Most of us did dead-end jobs in factories but outside the factory world you could be something better"

PAUL MATTHEWS
Skinhead, suedehead & mod since 1967, Wattstown

"My first memory of mod was around 1964 in Wattstown. There would be this group of lads that used to hang around on Enid's Wall. Enid's was a shop which had a wall outside with a little lip that they all used to sit on. They would be wearing John Smedley, Levis, monkey jackets or ice cream jackets. Some of them, like Ianto French wore parkas, but this was mainly when they rode their motor scooters. They loved listening to The Kinks. I remember them always talking about them and listening to them on the radio that they used to carry around.

"The most infamous mod in the whole of the Rhondda was Bomper Harris. He was from Wattstown and lived two roads down from Enid's shop. He was the first person I ever knew that went to Borstal and prison but he was always smart and always in suits.

"We moved to a part of Ynyshir called Mount Pleasant and five of us in the street were mods. Our road was split by an allotment – there were mods on one side and rockers on the other. It was like there was a constant war going on.

"The mods in Wattstown were different to the mods in Ynyshir. The Wattstown boys on a Friday night would go down to Pontygwaith and Ynyshir and then over to Porth to fight rockers. Ynyshir proper was full of rockers, apart from Mount Pleasant, which was all mod. The Mount Pleasant

I'm not like everybody else

"Our road was split by an allotment – there were mods on one side and rockers on the other. It was like there was a constant war going on"

mods were peacock mods so they tried to avoid trouble.

"By 1966 the skinhead side of things started to come in. I had a friend who was older called Keith Weaver. He was in the Merchant Navy. They would take me to the football as they had a car.

"I remember one match, Charlton at home it was, where we were in the enclosure and I could see all these boys with short hair and v-necks steaming across the Bob Bank, kicking and punching everyone. I asked Keith who they were and he said they were hard- or gang-mods and they come from East London. Two weeks later exactly the same thing happened – except it was Millwall this time. Of course, then Cardiff started to get their own skinhead gang.

"Mods tended to wear desert boots in Cardiff and the valleys mods wore Chelsea boots. Cardiff skinheads would wear grain-leather workman boots with the toe cap inside. The Valleys skinhead would wear pit boots with external toe caps and the hobnails.

"Aston Villa-Cardiff at home in 1969 we used railway bolts as weapons. We picked them up on the journey down from the Valleys. You could hear the Valley's skinheads coming off the train as they wore hob-nail steel-capped boots and there would be this noise as they approached the ground."

CAFÉ SOCIETY

"These cafés were doing a roaring trade in the 60s and were, of course, the perfect hangout for young mods"

Italian cafés were at one point as common in Welsh Valley towns as tea and cake. The locals called them 'Bracchis,' after the Bracchi family who are thought to be one of the ice-cream parlour pioneers in area.

In their hey-day, it is thought that there were over 300 of these eateries dotted across South Wales. They would dish out frothy coffee and steamed pies to miners before or after their shift and sweets and ice cream to the children after school.

This wave of Italian immigration began at the turn of the century and today Wales has the largest Italian community in the UK. Many of these Italians originated from Bardi in Northern Italy and came to settle in what were then thriving industrial valley towns.

These cafés were doing a roaring trade in the 60s and were, of course, the perfect hang-out for young mods. Who needed Soho when you had a decent coffee and a jukebox just down the road in Treorchy? Numbers may have now dwindled, but there are still a few of these cafés carrying a torch for this unique facet of Welsh culture that means the names Conti and Carpanini trip off the tongue as easily as Jones or Jenkins.

Opposite page: The Station Café in Treorchy owned by Domenico Balestrazzi, or 'Dom', who took over the cafe from his father Joe in 1965. Following pages: The Park View Café Pontypridd, with owner Peter Cruchi on page 51 (left).

I'm not like everbody else

I'm not like everbody else Café society

CHAPTER TWO

Days of change

Punk, power pop and new wave

"I spent an hour every night in my mother's front room trying to get the same sound out of the harmonica as Little Walter"

BRYN GREGORY
Singer and musician, Aberdare

Bryn Gregory was the lead singer and songwriter with Beggar, a Welsh mod band who made a name for themselves on the London mod scene in the late 80s. The band featured on the legendary *Mods Mayday* album of 1979 alongside the likes of Secret Affair and Squire. In 2011 Detour Records released *It Beggars Belief* featuring tracks from demos the band recorded at their base on Leyton High Road, East London.

"We moved to London because we wanted to hit the big time. We used to record demos, but record companies wouldn't even listen to them if you were from Wales, because Wales just wasn't cool. So we just upped-sticks and got this little flat in Walthamstow. Me and the drummer shared a bed-sit upstairs and the other two lived downstairs. We had to look through all our equipment to see the TV. The drummer was like the manager and got himself a job in an office where he could use the phone to ring people up for gigs.

"We were successful pretty much as soon as we went to London, because we were shit hot. We all got ourselves little day jobs and spent every afternoon after work rehearsing. We had a residency at The Saxon House in Walthamstow on a Monday night. All the mods in the area would turn up to this. So as well as our own songs, we'd always chuck in few Kinks or Who covers. It was good, because it meant that we improved as musicians as we had to work and learn the songs quick.

"I got a job working as a carpenter at Walthamstow Council. I remember walking up the road one night and it was pissing down with rain. I had my working clothes on

Days of change

"With Beggar – everything was up-tempo. If I wrote a ballad the boys would say: *Shut-up you soft bastard!*"

and was carrying my tool bag. I remember a load of mods shouting at me: *'Oi Bryn you don't look like a fucking mod today do you?'*

"We also played The Bull in Hornchurch and The Bridge House in Canning Town where the *Mods Mayday* album was recorded. We made a few mistakes on that recording. I blew a few bum notes on the harmonica, but we were all energy and I think the energy overtook the mistakes. If we had stayed sober and went straight on stage it would have had no atmosphere.

"We used to come back to Wales and do a few gigs but even though record companies were interested in signing us, we ended-up splitting up. Jeff the guitarist fell in love and left the band. We got another guitarist, but it was never the same. I ended up joining up with a guy from Cardiff to form The Co-Stars. We did a load of mod gigs – playing at rallies and that.

"Beggar was always fast RnB, while The Co-Stars were more soul and pop. I found that I could write songs differently in The Co-Stars, plus I finally learnt how to play guitar properly. With Beggar – everything was up-tempo. If I wrote a ballad the boys would say: *'Shut-up you soft bastard!'*

"I did the majority of the writing in Beggar, although Dave the bass player wrote *Broadway Show* which I think was one of our best songs.

"*It Beggars Belief* was released on Detour Records in 2011. The demos were recorded in a flat on Leyton High Road. Dizzy Holmes phoned me up out of the blue and asked if I wanted to put this stuff out. I told him I didn't have any reel-to-reel stuff as all I had were cassettes of what was recorded in the flat. We used to set up a mixing desk in the kitchen and mic the drum kit up in the living room and perhaps stick the guitar out in the kitchen as well and we'd rehearse. We'd record the rehearsal and that is what we would send to record companies.

"I was quite shocked that anyone wanted to put a record out after all this time. Back then we'd be banging on people's doors saying: *'Will you please record us?,'* and nobody wanted to know. So when 30 years later someone knocks on your front door and says: *'I want to release your stuff,'* it's quite bizarre."

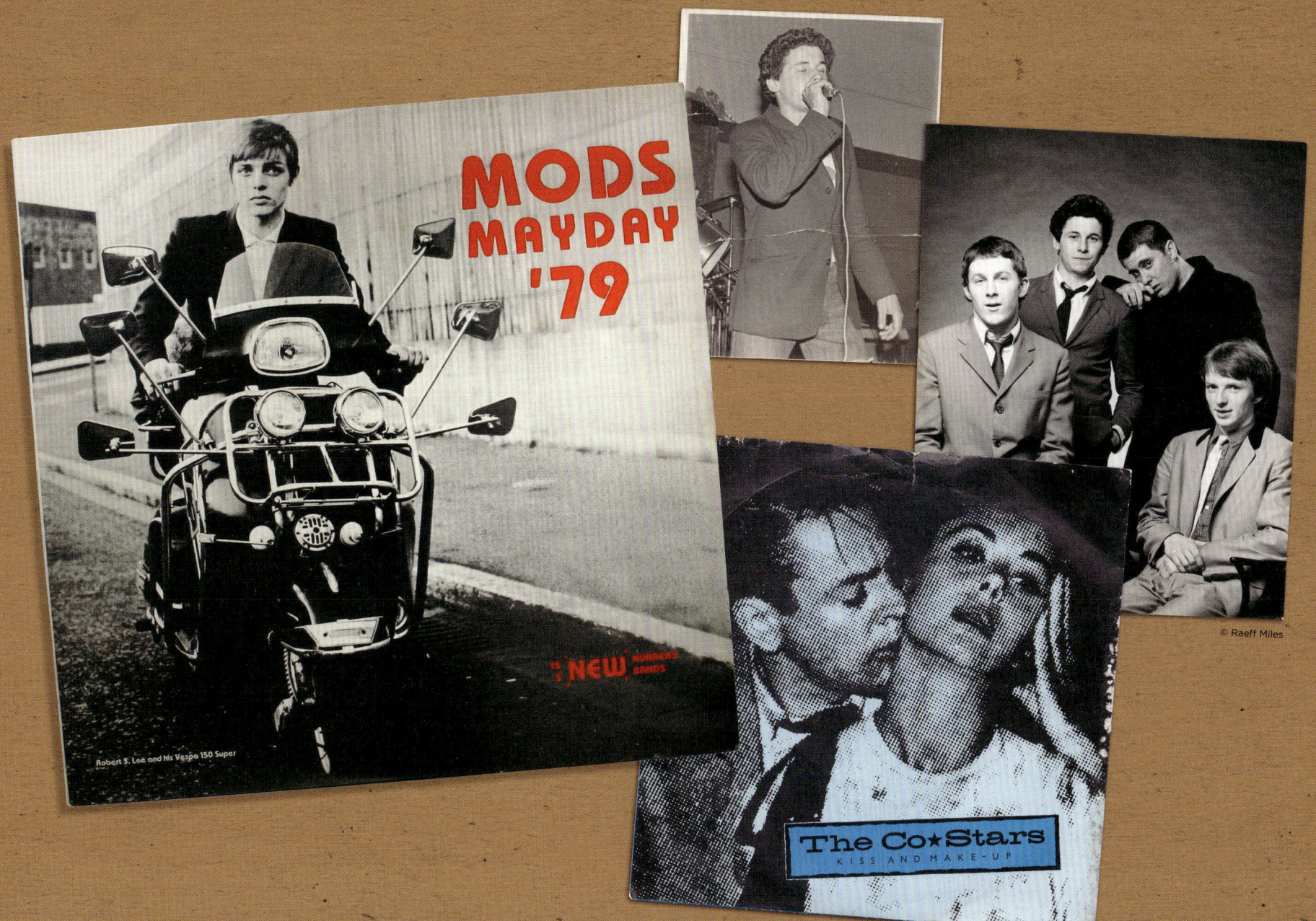

"They banned us in the end. We could buy take-out, but couldn't sit down. We were probably a nightmare"

CHRIS JONES
Park View Mod, Pontypridd

"There were very few places to go in Pontypridd. Park View Café was the regular haunt. That was once we all started to get scooters. We secured our pitch here by occupying all the available parking outside their establishment. We'd then fill up the seats in the café and order a coke or a coffee and a plate of chips between three of us. That meant no one else could sit down for a meal. They banned us in the end. We could buy take-out, but couldn't sit down. We were probably a nightmare.

"Prior to that we all used to meet up at a little youth-club in the United Church on Gelliwasted Road every Saturday night. We weren't a drinking crowd really, not at first anyway. The youth-club played all our records and allowed us the latitude and safety to express ourselves. It was a strange time for music. Loads of tribes. The club used to resemble a fancy dress party. Mods, punks, teds and skins, a load of normals - It was like Fraggle Rock some nights. No goths though. They were all up the graveyard drinking cider.

"The underground car park beneath the precinct was where we used to go when the club was closed and it was raining. It was dry and had a distinctly dark, menacing aura to it. A little bit New York/West Side Story. I can still hear the wind whistling. There were no nightclubs worth attending. We eventually gravitated to The Railway pub just outside the town centre. That's where the scooter club proper started.

"A few of the more adventurous types, Steve Garland, Mickey Knowles and myself, took to popping into Cardiff. Lloyds, under The Philharmonic, was a regular haunt. They did a sixties/mod/soul night there. It was a more authentic vibe than we were used to.

"I used to spend my Sunday mornings at The Seagull Café in Trecco Bay, Porthcawl. That's were I met Eddie Crole and the A48 Scooter Club members. A really hip crowd. They were my gateway to the joy that is Northern Soul. The dances at The Stoneleigh and The Manor Suite were legendary."

Days of change

"I always said: *I'm a mod in life, not just for weekends*. Excuse the cliche, but mod is a way of life"

MIKE KNOWLES
Park View mod, founder Pontypridd & District Scooter Club

ANDREW KNOWLES
'Top mod in Ponty,' Pontypridd & District Scooter Club

"I first got into mod around 1978 and used to go to Park View to look at the bikers. There would also be some boys on scooters down there and some friends from school – next thing we knew, we were all mods. I was about 14 at this time. We didn't see it as a mod hangout, but as time went on it became one.

"We used to wear parkas, two-tone suits and Fred Perry tops. We got our clothes from Michael Lloyd's in Taff Street, Stud Menswear in the precinct or the arcades in Cardiff. We used to go to Top Rank and Sophia Gardens in Cardiff and the Polytechnic in Treforest, where we saw The Jam, Secret Affair, The Chords, The Lambrettas and many more.

"To me mod gave us an identity and an attitude that stays with you for life. I think Park View was in the right place. It just got well known and we were all respected by others as we always stuck together. We didn't let each other down when there was trouble and it grew in popularity from there on."

"I was first introduced to mod when my brother Mike became a mod. Listening to *Glory Boys* by *Secret Affair*. Sitting on my brother's scooter outside the house. Even as a child I would wear Fred Perry and Sta-Prest trousers.

"I later became actively interested in the mod scene, buying my first scooter and going away on rallies. In particular we went to the Isle of Wight International scooter rallies. During the early 90s into the noughties were my favourite times. Me and my good friend, Grayson Davies, travelled together to various do's and rallies.

"We reformed Pontypridd & District Scooter Club, which at the time grew to be one of the most popular scooter clubs around. We originally met at the Pottery Pub on Treforest Industrial Estate, but we decided to try and return to as close to Park View as possible.

"Due to traffic and the large numbers showing up we opted to meet outside the Llanover Pub just across the way. Although we don't meet much anymore, there is still a large contingent of scooterists there on Tuesday nights."

Days of change

"A lot of my friends were surprised to see me with a Dobie Gray record in one hand and a Sex Pistols in the other. But I didn't see a difference, as it was just music to me"

LEWGI LEWIS
Scooterist and record collector, Porthmadog

"It was the song *Green Onions* that got me into the 'scene.' That one track just opened my eyes to a world of music. I'd saved pocket- and paper-round money to buy the Booker T and the MG's greatest hits and that started my obsession with records. I now own a few thousand.

"I was born in 1972, so it was the second wave mod/Two-Tone tone stuff I used to buy, which was always next to the punk stuff. So as I got older and had a bit more cash from birthdays etc, I'd go straight to Cob Records to spend it.

"I really enjoyed the punk energy and vibe so I kinda stuck on that side of the fence mostly but would dip my toe in 60s stuff too, like The Animals and The Who.

"Soul was a big part of my life growing up as I'm the youngest of six and there is an nine-year gap between my siblings and me. I remember records everywhere in our home. Most of them were left after my older brothers and sisters had left home. So I used to spend most nights listening to Martha Reeves, Marvin Gaye, Otis Redding, Oscar Toney Jr and many more.

"When I reached my teen years I had three or four weekend jobs so that I was earning enough to buy records on a weekly basis. I used to spend hours going through the second-hand section of the record shop. A lot of my friends were surprised to see me with a Dobie Gray record in one hand and a Sex Pistols in the other. But I didn't see a difference, as it was just music to me.

"I bought my first scooter at 16, then sold it to buy records. I got another at 19 and I have had one ever since. They've all been Vespas.

"I started the Madog Scooter Club (in Porthmadog) in 2015 and we quickly got like-minded people involved to help us create a 'rally' with soul djs and live music. We now hold rallies every year."

Days of change

"I paid £12, to get my nice long hair cut and went back on the train to Ffestiniog a mod"

WONG (EVAN WYN DAVIES)
Revival mod, Blaenau Ffestiniog

"In the early 80s the mod scene here was a mix of mods and soul boys. The elder souls boys used to go to Wigan Casino and the Winter Gardens, Llandudno.

"The Ffestiniog mods were Phil Jennings, David Hughes, Dylan Williams and the late Chris Jones (Chico Bach). We all went to the same school. They were all mad into The Jam and the Style Council, while I was a long-haired bass-playing rocker.

"In 1982 David Hughes and me went on the train to London to visit Chris (Chico) where he was training to be a nurse at Stanmore Hospital. First night there, we went to an all-nighter at the 100 Club, next day we went to Carnaby Street. It was an awesome experience, a real eye-opener for a Ffestiniog lad. I paid, I think, £12, to get my nice long hair cut and went back on the train to Ffestiniog a mod. To this day this story crops up now and again.

"We still kept in touch, going to Rhyl to meet and down to Cardiff to see David and Dylan. In 1987 David joined the Cardiff Cougars Scooter Club. I remember me, Phil and David going to see Prince Buster and Desmond Dekker down there.

"The mod scene in Blaenau Ffestiniog is still there, but the soul scene is getting bigger and bigger now in the North, which is great for meeting friends you haven't seen for years.

"My name is actually Evan Wyn Davies, but everyone even my mum, now calls me Wong. My friend Paul Owen gave me the name Wyn Wong because the woman next door to him was called 'Winnie Wong' because of her Chinese looks."

Wong (Evan Wyn Davies) **Days of change**

Wong (Evan Wyn Davies) and Mad Dog Scooter club founder Kevin Michael Tiernan

"**Before the internet this is how we learnt – from sleeve notes, from the *NME* or something on a hand-written flyer. You were always collecting these little pieces of information and it might take you years to find the connections between them**"

EDDIE CROLE
DJ & soul lover, Porthcawl

"My best mate at school was Dai Humphries and he was always into everything first. He came into school one day and he had a parka on and a farmer's hat which he had cut the rim off to make it look like a trilby. He stuck the hat on my head and said: *'Right Ed, we're mods now.'* I didn't even know what a mod was at that point."

"We used to head into Cardiff most Saturdays to meet at Asteys Café. When we weren't in there were were running around causing trouble and hiding in shops. At the time the police were putting things in the paper telling everyone to keep their kids at home on a Saturday because of all the trouble in town but all that did was act like a magnet for us all. Most of the mods were younger than the punks and skinheads – so it was boys to men. It was all frightening and exciting at the same time.

"I moved up to Aberystwyth when I left school. My parents ran inland arcades and piers and they had one up there which I went to work on. One of the guys up there was a mod in the 60s. He had a scooter and used to go to all the all-nighters.

"His big claim to fame was that he once had a pee standing next to Benny King in the Twisted Wheel. He told me all about the records. I'd started getting into 60s music by then. The Beatles first and then The Kinks. He also told me all about the drugs – the black bombers and purple hearts and this completely fired my imagination.

Eddie Crole **Days of change**

"When I was about 17 my dad's company opened up an arcade in Rhyl. I was desperate to get a scooter by this time but the nearest scooter shop was in Wrexham. So I got the Yellow Pages and found the number of the shop. They had a Lambretta GP 150 up there so I arranged to go and see it on the Saturday. I borrowed the money out of the safe without asking my dad with the aim of paying him back after. I then went round the second hand shop and bought a helmet that didn't fit and off I went on the bus and with the idea that I would be coming home on this scooter. But when I turned up in the shop, the guy there said it had been sold.

"So I asked where the next biggest town was – which was Chester. I got on the main road and thumbed a lift. In them days I knew that if I walked into a town on a Saturday I'd find a big gang of mods there. So I walked round Chester for about an hour and was just about to give up and get the bus home when I turned the corner and sure enough there was a load of mods. So I walked up into the middle of them and said: *'Has anyone got a scooter for sale?'* And one of them said: *'Yeah, but its not working but come back with me and we can sort it out for you.'* So they took it apart and got it working, but the side panel was tied on with string.

"They then explained that it needed petrol and oil but I was so excited that I'd be riding home on this scooter that I wasn't listening. Anyhow, I filled it up with petrol but didn't put any oil in. So there I am going up the road with the scooter kangerooing along with the side panel falling off every five minutes. I had no idea what I was doing. I had not tax or insurance.

"I was only up in the Rhyl for three months and by the time I left I'd ended up buying three scooters. The second one I bought was off a guy called Martin Lapin who was the top mod up there. He used to have a white GP. The scooter had *'Mr Ms'* on one of the side panels which was the name of the oldies room up at Wigan Casino and had *Okeh Northern Soul* on the other side. He was the coolest kid up there.

"When I came back to Porthcawl I started going to the all-nighters at Yate in Bristol. At the first one I remember I waited till 4am in the morning for the only record I knew, which was *Wade in the Water* by Ramsey Lewis. I was dressed in a tonic suit and tie and didn't know anything about the dancing – but gradually picked it up. I used to practice in my bedroom. Once I got into soul that was it. It was just so much more sophisticated than what else was around the time.

"Mod to me is about being open and not being closed. There are no rules. It's not just about the 60s and scooters. It's about nice design, getting the best of everything and being open to all cultures. In that way it has opened things up for me."

FANZINES

"Pre-internet days, fanzines were the main club guide, connecting mods all over the country"

ONE WAY WORLD
David Owens and Paul Macnamara

"My laughably stitched together fanzine *One Way World* (named after a Secret Affair song), was strictly second division compared to some of the glossily professional 'Premier League' ventures that served as the pinnacle of amateur publishing. However, my print rites-of-passage was symptomatic of the post-punk generation who aspired to 'do-it-yourself'.

"And so we did it ourselves, youthful enthusiasm far outweighing any sense of professionalism; a couple of hundred copies produced with love and passion. I threw mine together with Pritt Stick and Letraset. And it shows! The mum of my partner-in-crime Paul Macnamara printed it on a work photocopier, while the rest were copied at Prontaprint on City Road. It was sold at gigs around South Wales at venues such as the New Ocean Club and The Central Hotel, who hosted shows by the likes of The Truth, Small World, Makin' Time, The Moment and The Rage. It was also stocked in Buzz & Co (the original stockists of Jam shoes in Cardiff) the shoe shop in Castle Arcade. We also sold quite a few via mail order courtesy of the Phoenix List, a must-read (for any young mod at least) weekly newsletter linking up the movement at the time."
DAVID

"A trip to one of the legendary Ilford Palais Mod Alldayers, inspired lifelong friend Dave Owens and I to start writing our fanzine, *One Way World*. Pre-internet days, fanzines were the main club guide, connecting mods all over the country. Along with others such as *Fabulous*, *Pink Flamingo*, *Odd Issue*, *Take 5* and *This Is What They Want*, South Wales contributed to this nationwide network."
PAUL

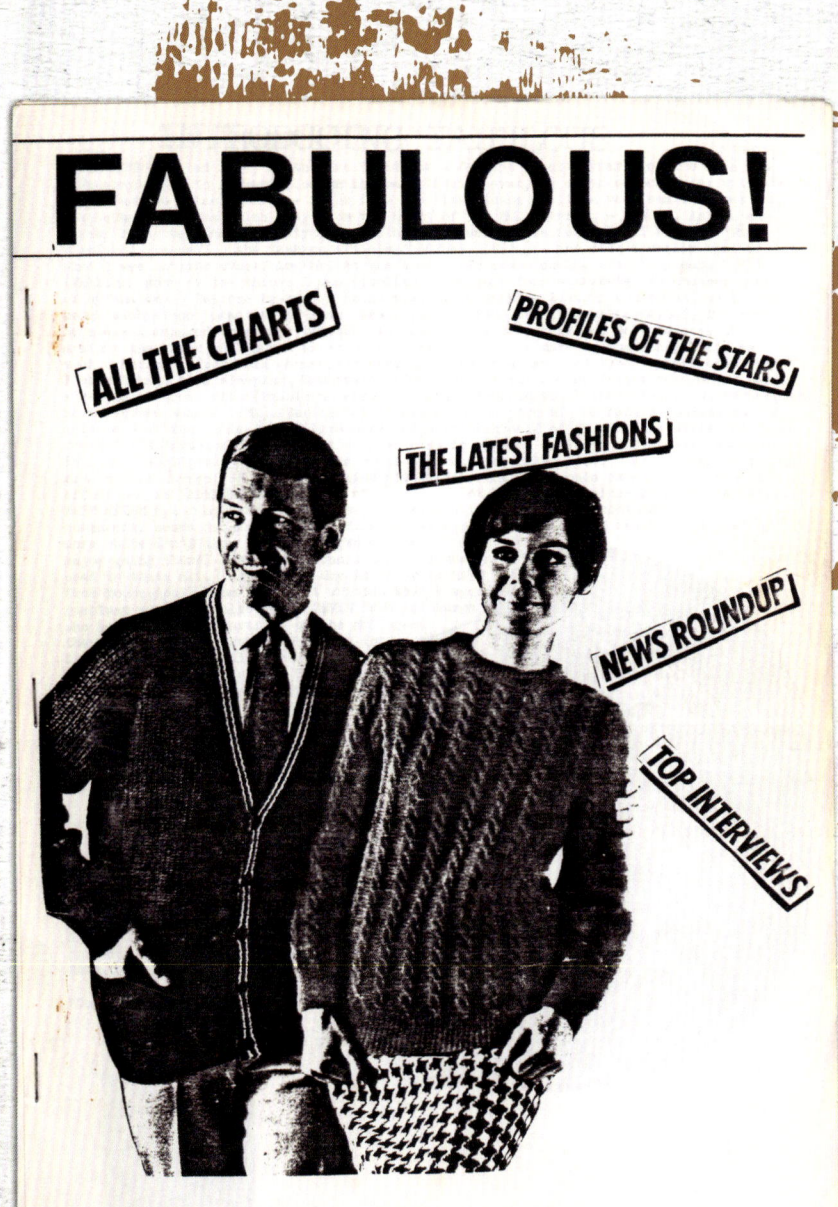

FABULOUS
Des Mannay

"It's impossible to overestimate the importance of 'Modzines' in keeping the scene alive. Once the music press decided we were past our sell-by-date, they pumped oxygen into a scene gasping for breath.

"The most important UK zines of the early 1980's in my opinion were Eddie Piller's *Extraordinary Sensations*, Ray Margetson's *Patriotic* and Janet Page's *The Way Ahead*. They were quality reads and the writing was always honest.

"I became firm friends with Ed (Piller) – but he was also a source for music and an evangelical mod. So we were mates before we even met. His letters would often end with *'go see this band'* or *'have you heard...?'*"

TAKE FIVE
Jane Williams

"The name came from one of my fave tracks that was being played in the mod clubs of the time. I mostly used items from 60s magazines, made up my own articles and included some of my pen-friends. I was writing to mods in Germany, Italy, Austria and Australia and we often swapped photos.

"I only did around 50 copies which were sold to some mates and through Buzz & Co – the shoe shop in Cardiff, which was where everyone put their fanzines. I only did two issues in the end. It was hard work. It was all done on my little type-writer with the photos stuck on the pages. All very *Blue Peter*. I'm glad I had a go and it still brings a smile to my face when I see a copy."

CHAPTER THREE

Saturday's kids

The early 80s and the end of the revival

"It was a bit like Moses going to the top of the mountain and getting the Ten Commandments off God"

STEVE GARLAND
Hairdresser, singer and general 'ace face', Ynysybwl and Elche in Spain

"I went to see *Quadrophenia* at the The White Palace in Pontypridd one day straight from school. I walked in one person and I walked out another. After that, I had my uniform altered, my tie made slimmer, my trousers taken in and buttons put on my shirt collar. Everything had to be adapted.

"It was a bit like Moses going to the top of the mountain and getting the Ten Commandments off God. When you are in the Valleys you aren't exposed to that sort of thing. It wasn't about wanting to be that person in the film – I was that person. So my DNA was mod without me even realising it.

"The most important thing for me was getting the first scooter because I didn't want to be a 'foot mod'. So when the scooter came everything else followed from that. I never really did the scooter rallies – staying in a tent and getting all dirty isn't for me really.

"My first scooter was a Rally 200. I was 17. I got it from a guy in Pontypridd who used to work for Barclay's Bank. My parents wouldn't buy it for me so I had a word with my nan and she gave me the money and I paid it off every week. We would always end up meeting outside The Park View Cafe and sit on the benches until the police or Peter the owner had had enough of us. We would sit all night drinking coffee and have the odd bag of chips. There was no alcohol or drugs involved.

"I got married 1987 and had a baby. So we concentrated on family life for a while, but then when Oasis hit the scene it changed for me again. I remember seeing something in a men's magazine about the Brit Pop thing and I phoned Jump The Gun in Brighton to get hold of the clothes and they invited me down for the weekend.

"It was then that I really discovered the 60s and all the other other hip stuff that goes with it. I started organising gigs and DJ'ing in places like Smarties and Modesty. Then I hooked up with Rob Bailey and started doing the door at their events. It was around that time that The Untouchables split and became The New Untouchables.

Steve with his wife Helen and Jeff Banks

"Rob was trying to make modernism attractive to people of different backgrounds and different mindsets. As long a people were dressed smart we didn't really care where they were from, or what music they were into. We never wanted to be like anyone else – The New Untouchables was the epitome of the new modernism in the 21st century. All these other little splinter groups think they are doing the right thing, but they are just going over old ground that we left over 20 or 30 years ago.

"Rob Bailey opened my eyes to stuff I'd never heard of previously. On a monthly basis Rob would send me 50 odd records, or they would be waiting for me on the door of the venue with a note: *'Records for Steve Garland'*.

"We would travel down to Brighton and London in the Mini. I've had my Minis for over 30 years. I remember taking the Mini to the Isle of Wight with the Lambretta on the back in the trailer. I pulled into a service station and there were a load of guys from Liverpool there who were taking the piss because I hadn't ridden the scooter down.

"I said to them: *'For me its not about driving as far as you can on a scooter. I'm a mod and that Mini is full of clothes. I haven't even decided what I'm going to wear yet. There are probably 20 pairs of shoes, 20 suits and 60 shirts in there and that's because I'm on a mod weekend. Whatever you're doing, good luck to you. I'm not interested.'"

Saturday's kids Steve Garland

"Yes you can buy the clothes, the scooters and even the records, but if you don't know what it's all about then you are wasting your time and believe me it shows"

CARL GRISLEY
Cascade, Bargoed

"For me – out of the three elements that I believe make up the mod genre: clothes, music and scooters – the scooter is the most important, followed by music, then the clothes.

"I would not call myself a mod – I'm more of a revivalist. I love the revival period and the bands from it. I get annoyed when so-called mods turn their noses up at it because, to be honest, if it wasn't for this period when we were younger, they wouldn't be mods today. Nobody got into 60s RnB, soul, jazz straight way. They first found the revival, and mainly The Jam, and then through finding out what influenced those bands, their interest in other eras grew.

"I have three scooters (at the moment). A 1959 GS150 Vespa (a Belgian VS5) fully restored, a 1963 TV175 Series 3 Lambretta, a 1981 Vespa P200e (Little Boy Soldier) and a 1956 Lambretta 48, which is currently under restoration. The scooters have won numerous trophies. Some of the ones I am most proud of include: 'Best Lambretta at Modstock – 50 Years of Mod', 'Best Vintage Vespa at Isle of Wight International Scooter Rally', 'Best Vintage Vespa at Antwerp International Scooter Show', 'Best Mod Scooter at Tenby National' and 'Best Vintage Vespa at Hayling Island Rally'.

"We do a lot of international rides because you can practically guarantee nice weather and because British rallies are not what they once were. Nowadays there are too many rallies on at the same time, so attendances can be poor, unlike in its heyday in the mid 80s, when the National Rally was just that - one national on that weekend. Lastly, when you go abroad, the people appreciate you making the effort and really look after you. We have made some great friends in Belgium, Italy and France.

"Mod is a mindset. You can't buy the memories, the friendships and the experiences we had growing up."

"The ironic thing was we were fighting kids that on the Monday we were sat next to at school"

PAUL 'SAMMY' THOMAS
80s mod and man-about-town, Newport

"Punk was the thing at the time which I never really liked. But then I got into The Jam and that changed it for me. Weller – his influence, his energy, his lyrics. When I was 13 I got my first two-tone suit for my birthday. That was it, I was smitten.

"When the film *Quadrophenia* came out, it was a double bill in the cinema. I remember being so chuffed getting in as it was an 18 and I couldn't have been more than 14 or 15. That film had a massive influence on me then so, of course, the next thing was having a scooter.

"I used to live in my boating blazer with white Levis and desert boots. There was a pair of trousers I bought in Nippers – the shop that Steve Strange used to own. They were skin-tight striped spearmint and I used to wear them on my Vespa 50 with a pair of canvas high tops.

"We would all meet in The Princess Tea Rooms in Newport by the train station on a Saturday afternoon and cause havoc fighting with the the skins.

"I remember one famous brawl in Roxy Records, which was the main record shop in Newport at the time. There was probably about 40 of us and over 200 skinheads and they all cornered us in there and it kicked off big time. The whole place got smashed up in the end and even made the *Newport Argus*. The ironic thing was we were fighting kids that on the Monday we were sat next to at school."

Paul 'Sammy' Thomas **Saturday's kids**

"Mod for me is a youth movement. It's about moving on not getting stale. It's about doing things right"

DARREN & JUNE LUKER
Ystrad, Rhondda

"June and I met in work. She was into Blur and Indie music which I thought carried the mod torch through the 90s and after a few 'liveners' in the Slug and Lettuce, we got chatting and that was it – 25 years later and she still hasn't stopped!

"I've always dressed casual in polos and knitwear - always Levi's and desert boots. You can't wear your suit popping down the motorway on a scooter, so I dress in protective gear for that. We are often camping on the rallies so the suits stay at home. I take my hat off to the faces that always look immaculate, fair play.

"I'm from a small village in the Rhondda we had a massive mod contingent there. The local motorcycle shop was a Lambretta main dealer, so scooters have always been about for me since an early age."

"I bought my first scooter when I was 15. It was a Vespa 150. When I was legal to ride I bought a Lambretta LI 150. I currently have a Vespa GS 160 – I think it's the icon of mod scooters. I have a Motovespa GS 150 Spanish GS, a Lambretta SX 200 and an auto Vespa GTV 300 which I use for long distance runs. June rides a Vespa et4 125 and my youngest son has a Vespa PK 50.

"Once you've been bitten, there's no going back. My mother and father had a record player and lots of vinyl including Trojan and Motown stuff. So when they went out Saturday nights I'd have the record player to myself and even though I never knew it then, it was always the same records I'd go back to again and again.

"Brighton is the pilgrimage for me. It's superb, even if you do get the 'comedy' element on the front. It's where you end up in the nights that set you apart from the rest. Sunny afternoons sipping coffee and watching the scooters go by – I love it.

"I also love the youngsters now taking up the reins, looking sharp and enjoying themselves. Mod for me is a youth movement. It's about moving on, not getting stale and just wearing 80s badges and flags. It's about doing things right."

Saturday's kids

"Punks, mods, rude-boys, we all had so much in common, we wanted to be different, have our own identity and voice but us mods just did it with more style"

MIKE CALUAN
Revival mod and clothes addict, Barry

"I love the theatrical aspect of the clothing, the look – that's always been a big thing for me. It's a way of expressing yourself individually, but at the same time belonging to a group of elite individuals. A band of brothers and sisters, an extended family. Also, there's the unspoken competition, to be the first to wear a certain thing or style, to discover the latest tune or quirky dance move, to emulate the style and attitude of the bands we loved and followed.

"To be honest, without all this, the sense of being part of something that made me feel alive, I don't know whether I'd be here now. To my teenage self there was nothing cooler, sharper or more meaningful.

"By the time I was 16, I had 18 suits, only two of them I bought from Carnaby Cavern in Newburgh Street, Soho – the rest were from charity shops. We'd pick them up for pennies. Three-button gems in every colour and fabric, from shark-skin tonic to linen. Looking back on it, the late 70s weren't that long after the mid-60s heyday of the Italian style (bum-freezer) suit and we reaped the benefits of those pioneering modernists' discarded memories and fashion trends.

"We lived on a diet of Oxfam, the Skin Shop and Astoria Sports – we'd get our Sta-Prest and jean jackets from the Skin Shop, while Astoria Sports in Barry was one of the only places that sold Fred Perrys. All the mods and rude-boys shopped there. The Fred Perry was a common clothing bond between us, as some rude-boys went as far as having the Laurel Wreath tattooed on their left chest. Now that's brand loyalty!

"We were like little wide-eyed magpies looking for anything and everything that resembled the look we were after. Basically, we wanted to emulate our idols. One of my favourite casual outfits was my white Levi jeans and jean jacket with a red turtle-neck jumper. I saw Keith Moon wear it on a poster of The Who and just had to find the look. I remember going up to Carnaby Cavern to get a suit made and you'd see all these young mods in there looking for the same shirt or scarf that Paul Weller had worn the week before on *Top of the Pops*, in The Jam's *Funeral Pyre* video.

"The plan was for a small gang of us to save up enough money to catch the 5am National Express to London and blow all our cash on a new suit, shoes and rare records. All this could be found in-and-around Carnaby Street, High Street Kensington Market (Sweet Charity) and sometimes Camden Lock. Now all this was back in the day before the high street chains got a strangle-hold on Soho… you could still find small independent shops and markets to meet your modernist appetite. Sad really that Carnaby Street has become a victim of its own success. Now it is more likely to be slated as a cliché than loved for its history.

"Once back home, we would sport our recent purchases like the 'boy about town,' strutting up and down Holton Road with a new suit, shoes and an attitude like the proverbial peacock. We thought we were chocolate and didn't care what others thought. The high street was our catwalk and we were out to impress.

"Closer to home, there was a little charity shop at the end of the High Street in Barry, where I discovered a whole tray of tie pins, collar pins and cufflinks in the window. It was like gold. They twinkled in the light – all shades and colours to add the finishing touches to any suit, shirt and tie. And to top it all, the woman let me have the lot for £1.50! You would never get that now. It wasn't called vintage then, it was just second-hand, something discarded that you found.

"Weekends were spent fliting from Nick and Terry's café on the Holton Road, or milling around Barry Island fairground dressed like an exhibitionist. Living on a diet of cappuccino, chips and consuming soul, blues and cherry-picked chart music. The Small Faces were always the band I identified with the most, as their style and attitude had a resonance with how and where I grew up. There was something cool about the fact that they never really went mainstream. They were a genuine mod band that showed us the way and influenced so many of the bands we all grew up with. The biggest compliment that anyone could pay you was that you had just stepped out of the 60s.

"Lots of the things we did back then would be perceived as being a bit of a cliché now. But it was all just being invented then. In hindsight, we were lucky in that we could pick different styles from different periods in the late 50s and swinging 60s. We had the freedom to pick a pair of shoes that were in style in 1962, a shirt from 1967 and a jacket from 1965 and make it our own style. It was exciting, it gave you your own identity. When I look back at that time, it was a period when youth culture seemed ahead of the fashion and music game. A musical and style-driven youth philosophy, tribes with their own look, musical taste and attitude. Punks, mods, rude-boys – we all had so much in common. We wanted to be different, have our own identity and voice – us mods just did it with more style."

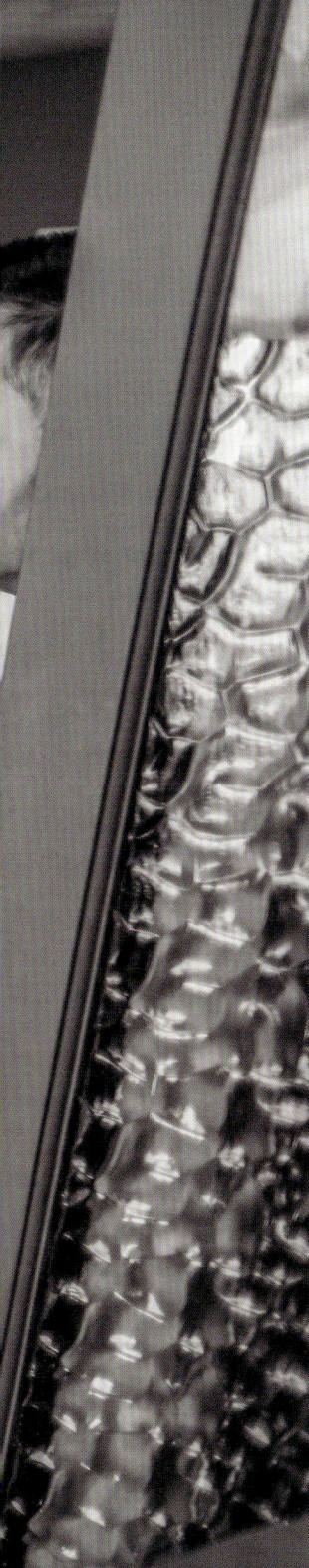

"If I had a time machine I'd go straight back to the jumble sales of the 80s. They were full of 60s clothes"

JANE WILLIAMS
80s mod, record collector and dancer, Neath

"Cardiff was a great place to be a mod. After the club Lloyds closed, we took over any club which had a 60s night. Monroe's and Fatso's spring to mind, although Fatso's didn't last long, as it got raided and shut down by the police. There were also regular pubs where we used to hang out, the Rummer Tavern was one and the downstairs bar opposite.

"There was also the pub on the corner of Caroline Street which was a real spit-and-sawdust place (literally had sawdust on the floor). You had to make sure you went in the lounge as the bikers all hung out in the bar. The jukebox was brilliant though, which was why we used to hang out in there. For bands, you couldn't beat the Top Rank – all the bands played there, it was fantastic.

"When a friend moved to London, she introduced me to the London scene and the Tony Class discos, which I thought were amazing. The first time I went, we were out Friday night after she finished work, Saturday lunchtime, Saurday night, Sunday lunchtime and Sunday night – all to different clubs. I went home totally exhausted. You literally could go out every night in London. Cardiff never quite reached that level!

"I remember looking at how much longer the skirts were. In Cardiff we were all still wearing minis. The smart mod era was very different, a bit more serious. They had a better idea in London of what the original mods were all about. I got a bit like that in the 80s as well. I didn't want to hang around with someone wearing a parka and Jam shoes. We felt that we've done that and moved onto something smarter which was closer to the look of the original mods."

"There was a big split around 1982 as a load of people became scooter boys and in a way it got rid of the rough element and just left the people who were proper mods."

"There was a big split around 1982 as a load of people became scooter boys and in a way it got rid of the rough element and just left the people who were proper mods"

lads showed me the basics of how to ride it, and I used to get up and practice driving at 6am so that the roads were quiet. My next scooter in 1982 was the small-frame Vespa Primavera 125. You either got old scooters from old men's sheds if you were lucky, or from Wares.

"Buying vinyl is something I've done since my early teens, although the music has changed along the way. There was never much money around, so the collection was always changing – especially in school/college. I used to sell old stuff so that I could buy new records. I'm not too fussy about labels. I just buy records I like."

"If I had a time machine, I'd go straight back to those jumble sales in the 80s, which were full of 60s clothes. In the last four years I've only managed to find two suits that fit (and that was after altering the skirts), I had loads of different ones in the 80s.

"I also wore my ski pants to death. I had about 12 pairs. Bought them all in jumble sales. There was only one charity shop that I knew of and that was in Roath in Cardiff. I'd be dragging out bin bags full of 60s ski pants, dresses, jackets.

"My first scooter was a Lambretta Jet 200 – nice idea but not good when you're a skint student. One of the

Saturday's kids Jane Williams

CHAPTER FOUR

Shadows and reflections

The written and spoken word

"If I hadn't been a mod I wouldn't be doing what I do today. It changed me completely. I always knew I would never be a 9-5 man. I wanted to try something else and that is what mod did for me"

JONATHAN OWEN
Writer, director, actor, producer, Merthyr Tydfil

"My older brother was a punk and he would let me into his bedroom and play his records to me. He was always really good at sharing stuff. At a very young age I heard the Sex Pistols and The Clash and all the great punk bands. But then he brought *All Mod Cons* by The Jam home and that blew all the other stuff away.

"We had *Quadrophenia* on VHS and my brother also had some *Ready Steady Go!*'s on tape, which I used to watch over and over again. I was probably about ten at the time. I was like one of those junior mods. I had lots of badges, a fishtail parka from Ponty Market, Fred Perrys, Ben Sherman shirt and Levis jeans. It was a long way away from the gorgeous suits of the late-50s that the early mods would wear. But the revival was so much more influenced by punk.

"By the age of 12 or 13 I was a proper weirdo and going to school talking about *Somebody Stole My Thunder* by Georgie Fame. The kids at school would be like, '*What are you on about? We are into Level 42?*' It's funny, because now all these people realise just how good the music was – particularly the likes of The Jam.

"I went to a reunion recently and the two most popular songs of the night were *Geno* and *Town Called Malice*. And I remember watching everyone and thinking – '*none of you would have fucking danced to this 30 years ago*'. So mod won really.

"Because Merthyr was a skinhead town you had to be constantly on your guard. I was always ducking and weaving about. I was like Welsh fly-half Phil Bennett with a side-step. There were a few times I got chased but I

didn't really get beaten up. I think, because I was only 12 or 13, rather than 15 or 16, I got a little more leeway than the older mods. Pontypridd was safe though, because it was a mod town and they had enough numbers to fight back. The danger for us was when we had to go back to Merthyr.

"It was a natural mod progression for me to evolve into the casual side of things. There is not a big jump between being a mod and dressing really smart and running round the beach at Brighton to dressing smart and going down the football on a Saturday. I remember the irony of seeing these really hard-looking casuals with wedges and jumbo chords dancing to the sweetest soul songs.

"I was in a band called The Pocket Devils in the early 90s. Trouble was, we were saying we were a mod band, which was career suicide at the time. People always told us not to say it, but we did it unashamedly and I'm quite proud of that. Then, when Blur famously came out on that *NME* cover with the headline – *'Touched by the Hand of Mod'* – that changed everything and suddenly everyone was saying they were a mod band again.

"We certainly had to work harder as a band in the Valleys. The guy who signed The Pocket Devils once said to me, *'I always prefer to sign a band from Merthyr than from London.'* The reason being - there was nowhere to play - so you would be rehearsing constantly and be piping hot. There was a pub by us called The Bell View, which used to put on country-and-western bands and that. We tried to get a gig there and as soon as we said we played our own stuff the manager went: *'Oh no, we can't have that.'* He agreed in the end to let us on if we played three covers. So we played something from The Stones, something by The Who and something by The Pretty Things and it was mobbed in there. So then, he was like, *'you can come back every week If you want.'*

"Me and Martin Freeman were having a chat after he'd seen the virals for *Svengali*. I said to him: *'What is it about west London mods? You can't win against these lads.'* They seem to think that be a mod you have to be born in a certain place and at a certain time. It is almost like the aristocracy of mod. Of course, I wish I could have been at Ronnie Scott's in 1958 but my father was only 17 years-old then! Whoever that Jewish kid was who walked down Frith Street in a beautifully-cut suit in 1958 – he's the first and only mod then ever – according to their argument. Of course, everything that has happened from that is going to be a dilution – but that's fine isn't it?

"I like to think that I live my life in a mod way and a with a mod ethic. Mod has informed me, not just in a fashion sense and in a musical sense, but in how I behave. The way I look after myself all comes back, I think, to being a mod."

Shadows and reflections Jonathan Owen

"There is a certain something about mod that simultaneously facilitates both a nostalgic looking back and a restless drive to move ever onwards"

PETER JACHIMIAK
Writer and academic, Neath

"I spent my childhood on a council estate in Cimla just outside of Neath. My father was a Polish immigrant and was a blue-collar worker all his life. As part of his naturalisation process he had to do heavy industry so he worked at the aluminium works in Rheola.

"We never had much money and my dad would bring his wages home in a brown packet and tip it out on the table. I remember he was constantly collecting scrap metal to take to the scrap metal merchants. He would then get a load of cash back and that would pay for Christmas.

"Back in July 1982, I somehow managed to convince my father to sit through an entire episode of *Top of The Pops* with me in order for me to watch The Jam perform *Just Who Is The Five O'Clock Hero?*. When they came on, it was an uncomfortable couple of minutes for us both: for my father, it was probably just a load of noise; for me, it was the moment where a leading band of the mod revival were at the peak of their powers.

"Squirming with inner, nervous energy (whilst being unable to release it in front of a parent), my father just muttered something under his breath about the young Paul Weller having "an expression of a boxer". It was, however, both the first and last time that I shared a moment of intimacy with my father over three minutes of popular music as just a few months later (after a very short period of illness), he passed away. He was 56, and I was 16.

"Thereafter, perhaps as a means of filling the huge void in my life, I immersed myself fully in mod, buying up (both at full retail price, and second-hand) bowling shoes, paisley shirts, boating blazers, and so on. However, with no bread-winner in the family any longer, times were tough for a teenage mod in an economically depressed

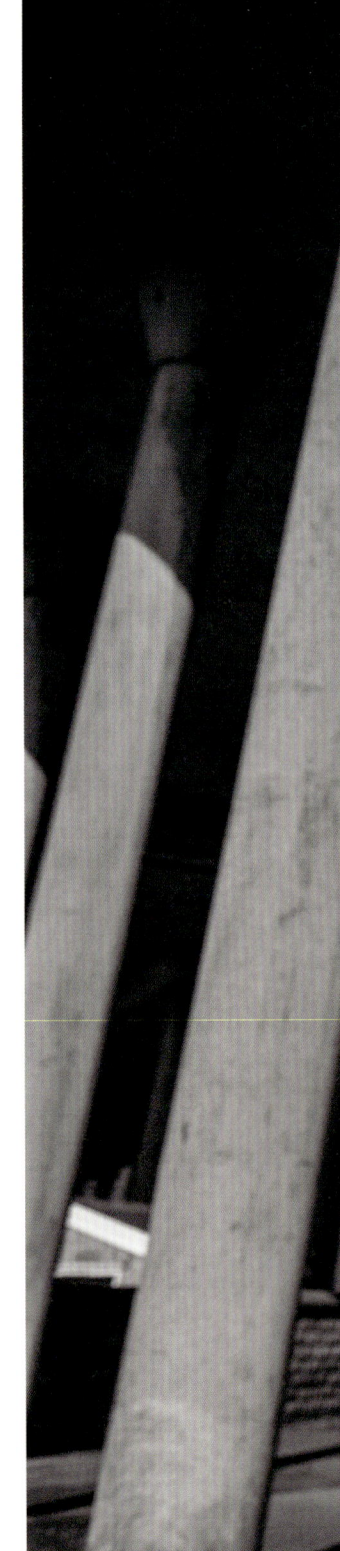

> "You got used to the hard stares, and the snide comments. I just lived for the moment when a local 'Face' would give you a nod of approval, and – looking you up and down would mutter the words: *Tidy, mun*"

south Wales, and my abiding memories of the time are of trudging the dark, rain-washed back streets of Neath town centre, dressed up to the nines, with a soggy girlfriend in tow.

"However, it was very much that obsessive endeavor to be constantly well-turned-out amid the drabness of Welsh life of the time that, to me, emphasised that I was living Peter Meadon's mod dream – that of *'clean living under difficult circumstances'*.

"And, boy, it didn't get any more difficult that being an out-of-work young mod in Wales during the Thatcherite 1980s.

"Yes, you did bump into like-minded – and identically dressed – stylish souls in Wren's Wine Bar, Windsor Road, Neath, but the majority of the bitter-drinking, rugby-supporting locals just thought we were odd-looking bods, who were both out of place, and out of time. Saying that, you got used to the hard stares, and the snide comments. I just lived for the moment when a local 'Face' would give you a nod of approval, and – looking you up and down would mutter the words *'Tidy, mun'*.

"We were very open as a family to Europe – for obvious reasons with my dad being Polish. So from a very early age I felt European and in a way, my 'modness' was always a reaction to two things: White, working classness and all its prejudices and ironically a reaction to Welshness – or what I saw at the time as the narrow mindedness of Valley life.

"To me mod and its embracing of scooters and coffee machines was everything I wanted to be."

"Mod is like a psychiatric diagnosis – it'll always be with you. It's not just for Christmas…"

DES MANNAY
80s mod and poet, Cardiff

"Mod was massive in the early 80s and there were plenty of gigs to go to. Venues such as The Top Rank in Queen Street, Cardiff would put on the odd Tamla Motown 'disco' and there was also the weekly 'Mod Mecca' in Cardiff at Lloyds every Sunday, playing a mix of just about anything that could pass as mod – 60s soul and pop music, revival stuff, Two-Tone, 60s ska and reggae – you name it.

"Unfortunately Lloyds closed its doors to mods after a group of scooters were set on fire in the multi-storey car park opposite the venue. It re-opened to mods twice more in the early 1980s. Initially on a Thursday night and eventually back on a Sunday. When Lloyds closed in 1981 some of us found another club, Monroe's, to hang out in, and there was also the psychedelic club, Café a Go-Go, run by James Parker and a couple of other people. There were also numerous scooter club do's – these were still 100% mod at the time. Also South Wales Soul Club started having 60s and rare soul nights in Porthcawl. And that's what they were called then – not Northern Soul.

"In terms of youth subcultures, which is where mod started out, our opponents were the world in general, and the nearest rival gang in particular. In South Wales terms, this led to the 'Cardiff Mod riots' of 1980; which went on for over a month every weekend.

"The *South Wales Echo* went into overdrive; reporting clashes between 300 mods and rockers in the first week, (to be fair - we did lay siege to a motorcycle exhibition. It was a bit provocative…). After that, the local punks decided to step into the rockers' shoes so there was at least another three weeks of rioting. *'Police fear bloodbath'*, the *Echo* opined. Yep, we were too impatient for all that bank holiday beach fight bollocks.

"Cardiff always had a big live music scene, and amazingly there were a few great local 60s soul outfits that mod's could check out by 1982 – namely Dansette (later Madassa Soul Band), and Laverne Brown. Laverne was described in *'Time Out'* magazine as 'Britain's Otis Redding' – he really was THAT good. Between 1982-83, a number of bands emerged. The most visible of which

Shadows and reflections

were The Colours from Newport; who used to busk regularly to huge crowds in Queen Street, Cardiff, as well as playing numerous gigs. They produced one single, *The Dance* on Loco Records and an album only available on cassette. Other bands on the scene at that time were, The Co-Stars, The Limit (from Newport), Local Hero, Street 66, Kaleidoscope (also spelt Kalidoscope), who were a local psychedelic band, Shake Some Action and No Mean Feet. The Co-Stars, of course, were huge in terms of local mod-oriented bands.

"Not only did they include Bryn Gregory, from Beggar, (one of the more promising acts on the '*Mod's Mayday 79*' album), but their output was prolific – a live album, 12 inch EP and a track on the first Countdown records compilation. Street 66 also produced a single, *Conman* on Loco records, and Shake Some Action recorded a demo tape on Loco which was never released. When Street 66 and Kaleidoscope split, some of their members formed the band A Sound Reaction with ex-members of another local band, The Hope. They joined the gigging scene and had a track released on a local compilation.

"The Lions Den underneath The Great Western Hotel was a bikers hangout. And when I say bikers, I don't mean a few Status Quo fans in denim jackets – I'm talking a seriously dangerous motorcycle gang. But Mondays were a bit quiet – so the manager booked one of 'our' bands. So we turned up mob-handed, and amazingly, both disparate groups tolerated each other. And so 'Mod Mondays' were born.

"The mid 80s were absolute heaven. This was the point when all the kids who'd been keeping mod alive after it got dumped by the media got to shape the movement. Mod went through various phases in the 80s – The Revival, Psychedelia, Northern Soul, scooter rallies (rather than traditional bank holiday mod runs). We'd all been at the forefront of these changes on the scene, as they just kept reinventing mod and keeping it fresh/novel, but with each new turn another bunch of people would decamp into scenes that we'd coexisted alongside – but were separate from.

"It was around this time that we started listening to classic mod sounds. We had a scorched earth approach and wanted to take everything back to year zero. The surviving mods became ultra smart, ultra cool, the clubs were just for dancing – not getting pissed, rucking and spilling beer everywhere, and there was an explosion of Modzine's and new more stylish bands and mod became massive again. But this time the scene was ours. We had our own media. New fanzines like *The Hipster*, *Life After 66*, *Right Track*, and *The INSET* were great.

"Let me explain, those of us who in 1983 were beginning to listen to RnB rather than Northern Soul, were now speaking fluent Jean-Paul Sartre and Colin MacInnes. We were gobsmacked when we discovered *Absolute Beginners* was being turned into a blockbuster bloody movie – it was *ours* for fuck's sake. There was also a mini revolution going on in the jazz scene with great new acts coming through. For us, Courtney Pine was our own home-grown John Coltrane. This was all OK on the mod scene – not controversial.

"Between 1984 and 1986 I considered myself a London mod who happened to live in Cardiff. Mod was my life. I used to work 18 hours a day in some shit Wimpy bar. But I could go to London three times a week: visit a tailor, see a mod band at the 100 Club and go to Sneakers in Shepherds Bush every Sunday night."

Shadows and reflections Des Mannay

CHAPTER FIVE

Dedicated followers of fashion

Pysch, vintage and other stories

"I don't like the label mod, but I love everything about it. A pair of Levis, a pair of desert boots doesn't make you a mod. What does make you a mod is about going that extra mile – the way you carry yourself"

PAUL MANSFIELD

Owner of My Generation Vintage online clothing store, Newport

"Originally it was all about the music and the clothes. For me always they go hand-in-hand. During the late 70s early 80s I would go to jumble sales to source vintage 60s pieces to mix with the new threads that I had purchased. Trying to get authentic, individual 60s look was always important for me. My red denim jacket with dogtooth trousers was my trademark look.

"My trousers would usually be second-hand too, because they would be better fabric. I would wear them with suede shoes and used to carry a suede brush around with me. I used to get paisley shirts in the jumble sales and if they didn't have a button-down I would button them down myself. I would alter things so they were right.

"When the Style Council came out I moved into that 'Euro-mod' look. No socks or brightly coloured socks. But I have always loved the 50s and 60s 'Americana' look from the old movies to the likes of *Happy Days*. The original Ivy League look of chinos, button-downs, Harringtons and Bass Weejun loafers always seem so cool.

"My wardrobe and home is full of vintage furniture including sofas, lighting, tables, record players, radios, prints and pictures. I have always loved stylish interior furniture particularly the 50s-inspired Sir Terence Conran furniture that he designed for Habitat. I still own a few of his original pieces. I can't just wear the original clothes and have MFI-type furniture around me. Recycling is

Dedicated followers of fashion

> "I have always loved stylish interior furniture particularly the 50s-inspired Sir Terence Conran furniture that he designed for Habitat. I still own a few of his original pieces. I can't just wear the original clothes and have MFI-type furniture around me"

important for me, I can't bare the throw-away culture.

"From the late 90s I had planned to start my own business by taking my passion to another level. So I started selling vintage in 2001 and had three shops in different locations. Originally called Retrocentric, I changed to My Generation Vintage in 2015. I have been selling 50s, 60s and 70s interior pieces as well as clothes over the last 17 years.

"Whereas most just like to dress the part occasionally, I live the part as much as possible. I don't like the label mod, but I love everything about it. A pair of Levis, a pair of desert boots doesn't make you a mod. What does make you a mod is about going that extra mile – the way you carry yourself."

Dedicated followers of fashion Paul Mansfield

"I liked the thought that no one else dressed like me or listened to the same type of music"

JAMES PARKER
DJ, founder of Café a Go Go and retailer, Cardiff

"The punk side of things never appealed to me really. So when I saw The Jam on TV on *Top of the Pops* it was almost like it was meant to happen. Something just made me identify with them straight away. The following Saturday I got my mum to tell me where all the second-hand shops were and I got hold of this black, three-button suit, which she then altered for me. She took the trousers in as they were too wide. It didn't have a ticket pocket on it, but it looked smart and it fitted me.

"I managed to find a white button-down shirt and and bought a black skinny silk tie and my dad lent me his leather trilby hat. I remember standing down at the bottom of Roath Park to get the bus into town and thinking: *This is brilliant, there are people going past and looking and staring at me – this is what I want. I felt like the peacock strutting his stuff.*

"My first scooter called 'Red Fox' – I badgered my mum and dad for months and months and used to leave the Vespa catalogue lying around the house hoping they would notice. Eventually they took me down to Reg Braddick's in Cardiff to buy one.

"Went to see all the revival bands that came to play in places like the Top Rank and the New Ocean Club. But very soon I started going to London, as that's where I needed to go to get the clothes.

"The influence of going to London led to me becoming more interested in all the psychedelic stuff and a fascination with bright colours. Me and my friend Mike Vincent (Alfie) found this shop called The Regal in London and got quite friendly with the owner. It felt like quite a natural thing for us to do to keep evolving. We went to see a lot of bands in London and met some very weird and wonderful people. We even would get the train down to Brighton to visit clubs down there and end up sleeping on the beach.

"Even though I had only been into the mod revival for a few years, I always had the feeling of wanting to be different and one step ahead of everyone else. I had never heard any of the cliché mod quotes at that time of not being like everyone else etc, it was just something in me that wanted to keep moving, keep evolving.

"I liked the thought that no one else dressed like me or listened to the same type of music. My friend Alfie shared the same ideals. At 16 we were regularly on the bus to London, picking up all the latest mod fashion trends, mixing with people a few years older than us and

120   **Dedicated followers of fashion**

James Parker **Dedicated followers of fashion**

seeing how the mod scene there was moving so quickly with fashion and music.

"We went to various clubs, heard bands playing different styles of music other than soul and Motown and started to hang out at shops such as The Regal in Newburgh Street and Sweet Charity in Kensington Market, making great friends with the owners, the people that worked there and anyone who was passing by. We wanted a bit of this for Cardiff as well.

"We persuaded the likes of Hudson & Hudson and Robert Barker's to stock clothes from these stores. We set up our Saturday shop within Civilisation on one of the arcade balconies and decided we needed a club night to go with it. Mike came up with Café A Go Go and with the help of two people that were on the Cardiff club scene (Mark Taylor and Jinx) we found a venue. Armed with a clutch of tunes we had learned about from our London trips, a mix of late 60s British & American psych/garage and also new psychedelia bands such as Mood Six, and Playn Jayn we set about publicising the night.

"*The South Wales Echo* had got to hear about this new Cardiff scene and organised photo shoots of myself and a few friends all dressed up in our bright paisley colours, which all helped to get the night publicised. We had people queueing the whole length of the arcade trying to get in and had to turn many away. In the days long before social media this was a pretty cool achievement.

"We ran the night for I think three events in town and then had a change of venue to Mel's down Bute Street. I had moved to London then and it all started to drift away until 2006 when I revived the night under the soul/RnB theme. It was great fun and nice to look back on a time when we brought the 'New Psychedelia' to Cardiff."

"The thing is, you can't define a mod, but you can always spot an old one"

ADAM LEWIS
All-round dandy and psych lover, Swansea

"My Dad taped the film *Quadrophenia* for me when it was on the telly and from the opening credits I was hooked. I just thought – *'that's what I want'*. The whole look was fantastic – it was smart but quite subversive with it. This was the late 80s and there was nothing in Swansea at the time. There were the 'Townies' who went into Swansea on the weekend in their black trousers and white shirts and there were a few heavy metal pubs. But that really was it. I was the only mod in the village, so to speak.

"I remember being chased down the Kingsway and being called a 'poof' for wearing pink hipster trousers. I was never involved in any of the violence though, or part of any gang. I wasn't going to be paying £80 to get a pair of trousers made just to get them wrecked in a fight. For me it was about looking nice, listening to good music and riding scooters.

"I went to the Isle of Wight rally in 1993 with a scooter club in Fareham, near where I was living at the time. I remember there were a couple of boys standing outside a shop in candy-stripe hipsters with proper 'bowley' haircuts and I thought – *'you know what? I want some of that.'*

"I didn't wear suits at all really. I tended to wear hipsters and shirts. I took my inspiration from bands like the Fleur de Lys or The Creation. But I never followed a set look. I just wore what I liked. For example, I might wear a long pointed collar, a button down or even a tab collar if I liked the shirt.

"When I think of mod, I always think of the classic look from around 1963. There are always loads of arguments about mod – but mod as it originally was, only lasted a couple of years. If you look at the clothes the Small Faces were wearing by 1966 – it wasn't mod. Maybe a year earlier they were dressing like mods. But it changed and technically this is what mods should do – adapt."

"Music wise in the 90s I was a massive Prisoners fan.

Dedicated followers of fashion

Adam Lewis **Dedicated followers of fashion**

"I got my Lord John cape from a charity shop in Eastleigh near Southampton for £10. They thought it was an old police cape in the shop. I get hassle wearing the cape, but I don't care, because I know it looks bloody good"

I picked up an album by The Prisoners in 1989 purely on the strength of the picture on the front. It was the *Rare and Unissued* album and had a picture of Graham Day on the front wearing a white denim jacket."

"I remember finding a royal blue double breasted suit with a velvet collar and putting it on and enjoying the fact I had a slightly different look. Suddenly you might start wearing a paisley shirt with that, or a cravat or a tie. Even though it was a late 60s style, it was never a hippie look. It was always smart.

"For me Brian Jones' style sums that short period between 1966-1968 when people still looked smart but dandyish at the same time."

"Let's face it, I'm not the most conventional looking mod lad you'll ever bump into. I'm a bit of a wildcard I suppose. But those who know me know where I'm at"

SIMON QUINN
DJ and clothes fanatic, Gelligaer

"I've always been forward-thinking. I spend a lot of time, too much time in fact, in funk/soul nights, mod nights, house music nights. I'm lucky in that I get to knock around with some real sharp people from all of the above-mentioned scenes. They may not wear the mod badge (although some do), but certainly their attitude to working, buying clothes and listening and collecting good music is absolutely second to none.

"I'm still quite heavily influenced in some ways by the mod scene and I'm still constantly looking for and buying sports/Harrington jackets, good jeans and neat polo shirts. But I'm not 16 anymore and I'm a considerable amount heavier. Gone are the days when I can pull off a certain look.

"As much as I appreciate how things were, I find it's a struggle to compete with the nostalgia and the retro thing. With a small amount of effort and careful thought it's not impossible to develop and maintain your own individual style. These days I tend to stick to three maybe four, at the most, labels for the core of the wardrobe with the odd vintage piece thrown in and I'm quite religious with that. You get to know how things size up and how to wear them. I'm just as comfortable in good shoes as I am in my daps and, of course, then there's the hats...

"It ain't 1964 or even 1984. Times change, style changes. But your musical sense of direction won't steer too far from your beaten track. I grew up a mod lad from the Valleys. I never chose to be one – it just happened. I couldn't help it. But I sure as hell believe in it. I know a lot of people with a lot of good memories. I have them too. But for me some of the best mod memories could happen at tomorrow's party!"

Dedicated followers of fashion Simon Quinn

"So much energy came off that record I wanted to smash up my own bedroom. I played it over and over. Nothing had hit me like that before. I was hooked"

PHIL MATSELL
Mod since the late-80s, Merthyr Tydfil

"At 13 I saw a clip of the Small Faces on *The Word* singing *Itchycoo Park*. Even though their look was a grown-out mod one, they just looked so different to everything that was going on around me at that time and that difference really appealed to me.

"The following day I went to W H Smith and managed to get Itchycoo Park with Tin Soldier on the flip, on a re-release 45. I also ordered a Decca *A&B Singles* album while I was there. When my Mam saw what I had bought, she went up the attic and returned with carrier bags full of 45s. There were all sorts in there: Stax, Motown – bands like the Yardbirds and Zoot Money.

"I found *Sha La La La Lee* amongst them. So I sat cross legged on the floor and put it on my little portable record player. But I didn't like it, so I flipped it over and played the b-side - *Grow Your Own*. When I heard what came out of those tiny speakers I started levitating. It felt like my head was touching the ceiling. So much energy came off that record I wanted to smash up my own bedroom. I played it over and over. Nothing had hit me like that before. I was hooked.

"I first went to London with Simon Bendle for the Buckingham Palace run in 1986. It blew our minds and to this day it is still one of the best weekends of my life. I can vividly remember walking down the stairs of the Master Gunner on the Friday night, Mel Torme's *Coming Home* playing, a sea of back-combs and Gabicci's. It all just stuck a hook even deeper in us. I'd just turned 17 and

Dedicated followers of fashion

Phil's life-long friend, mod Gav Evans on his Lambretta

I was like a sponge, soaking it all in.

"By the late 80s, the revival may have burnt out, but there were still quite a few mods about in other valley towns. The Malpas Chaps in Newport and Richard McCarthy in Cardiff were putting gigs and do's on, keeping things going, so you would meet people there. Round the back of Ware's scooter shop was another place you would meet people and that is where I met life-long friend Gav Evans.

"Moving forward means everything to me. I feel it's mod in its purest form. By 1990 I was into indie as well as Acid Jazz, funk, soul, rare groove, disco and some hip-hop, as well as all the 60s stuff. From 1995 onward, I thought it was a fantastic time to be a mod, as it wasn't a dirty word anymore.

"Today I spend more money on new releases than I spend on old. I try and dress contemporary with a nod to the past. At my age, it's more about my style and how I wear it that matters to me. I try to appeal to the one who might get me, not the ones that never will.

"It's as much about my attitude to life – a never-ending quest for a record that hits me like *Grow Your Own*, or the perfect item of clothing, the right shoes or part for my scooter. I continuously think about records, clothes, scooters and can't switch off. The only thing that takes my mind off it is football, but it quickly turns back.

"I may not look how others expect me to look, a but as it says on Simon Bendles' headstone: *Cool is to set your own identity, sheep follow others*. Mod has given me the vehicle to do that."

Dedicated followers of fashion Phil Matsell

"I have been a mod for 41 years and will remain one always. I love everything it stands for"

LESLEY HERBERT
80s mod and vintage clothes lover, Cardiff

"It was 1977, I was 10 years of age, and I heard a song by The Jam on the radio. I was instantly a fan. Every fortnight I'd go to the local newsagent to see if any Jam songs were in the new edition of *Smash Hits*. Soon my bedroom wall was full of posters with the lyrics to hits such as *In the City* and *Strange Town*. I was witness to the mod revival in the late 70's, and spent my teens finding out more about this subculture and its meaning.

"At high school I was often in trouble for not wearing the correct uniform of navy and yellow. At 14 I wore black winkle-pickers, a black mini skirt, a white shirt and a black inch-wide tie. I adopted the thick black top-liner with the flick, which I still wear today.

"Our 'gang' were a mix of mods, skinheads and trendies. We'd all grown up together, but by 15 we dressed according to our preference, so the train to Barry Island every Bank Holiday was an interesting mix. We had to split up when we arrived there, but travelled back together and all talked and laughed at the same time about whatever 'antics' we'd gotten ourselves caught up in.

"1984, I was 17 and I met my first boyfriend who was a mod. I thought he was so 'cool' when he came to pick me up on his Vespa, wearing his big parka. My current partner, Simon, has a collection of parkas including an original M-51. We have a 1966 Lambretta in old English cream with twin burgundy seats. Simon's style is a mix of vintage and modern. He styles a quiff and wears brands such as Fred Perry, Merc, Gabbicci or Warrior.

"My choice of style is vintage 60s and I prefer to wear original clothing, which I mostly buy on eBay. I love the style of that era, as it was a time of innovation in women's fashion, introducing capri pants and the mini skirt. I particularly like the Space Age fashion.

"I have been a mod for 41 years and will remain one always. I love everything it stands for. The style, the music, the scooters, the people. It is 'A Way of Life' and should never die out."

"Keep the Faith...I have!"

Dedicated followers of fashion

"The scene is like being part of a different family"

GILLIAN FINNEY-RICHARDS
Revival mod girl, Ferndale, Rhondda

"I was brought up on 50s and 60s music and loved the 60s look. Being still at school at the time and not working, I wasn't able to buy lot of gear. I used to get my shoes from Buzz & Co in Cardiff. I would wear a black parka with St. James' check, to be slightly different from the others. We would meet everyone from the Valleys on a Saturday in Pontypridd.

"The scene is like being part of a different family. I've made life-time friends, some of whom I have known for over 30-odd years now. You're never judged on how you look or dance. You can be yourself. People in the scene are always there for you and if you don't get out to certain events on regular basis you're always greeted with open arms and welcomed when you do."

Dedicated followers of fashion Lesley Herbert and Gillian Finney-Richards

> "I often get people coming up to me and sharing their stories of life in the 60s and being able to have that connection and common interest with a different generation is quite special"

ABIGAIL RACHEL
Sports presenter and vintage enthusiast, Neath

"I first got into mod when I was roughly 18/19 years-old and trying to find my identity. I watched *Quadrophenia* and listened to the soundtrack. I instantly engaged with it and everything about it made sense.

"I get my clothes mainly from charity shops. It can be quite an arduous challenge, especially as someone who is allergic to shopping, but I have been incredibly fortunate to find and fill my wardrobe with all original clothing… along with a few, quite a few, football shirts!

"My main style icons are Twiggy, Peggy Moffitt, Mary Quant and Edie Sedgwick. I would also say my auntie Katie had a big influence on me. Her 1960s' look, seeing her stand out from the crowd and not feel the need to be conventional taught me a lot.

"To be honest, I don't pay a lot of attention to the way people react to my image anymore. I spent a lot of my childhood severely lacking in confidence. I had no identity and was confused about what I enjoyed. Now I have found a subculture that represents who I am as a person. One thing I've found is that my appearance is a very good conversation starter, especially with people who were part of the mod scene the first time around.

"I think it sums it up that being a mod is a way of life. It's not a fad or a phase, you feel it in the heart. It's

Dedicated followers of fashion

To be honest, I don't pay a lot of attention to the way people react to my image anymore. I spent a lot of my childhood severely lacking in confidence

a passion and something to be proud of. I hope I look as good as they do on a scooter when I'm older!

"Music is such a significant part of my life. I listen to the majority of it on vinyl because, well, everything sounds better with a bit of crackle, right? I still remember the feeling I had when I listened to The Who – *I'm One* for the first time. I was able to relate to it instantly and the lyrics were quite appropriate to being a mod at a time when society constantly seems to make you feel like you are inferior for not conforming to what it deems an ideal.

"I spent the majority of my childhood in and out of psychiatric units being treated for various mental health conditions. I nearly lost my life on a number of occasions through both anorexia and depression. During this time I was so disengaged from myself and my interests - I lost my identity. The power this song had was incredible. It made me feel something.

"It's amazing how you can engage with a piece of music, how it can make you feel less isolated and that's exactly what *I'm One* did for me. It helped shape me as a mod."

Dedicated followers of fashion Abigail Rachel

THANK YOU

These are the people who backed the *Kickstarter* campaign to fund the research, writing, photography, editing, design, art direction and printing of this book. Without them this book wouldn't exist. Thank you to and everyone of you.

Adam Lewis	Gillian Richards	Margaret Bridgeman	Paul Slaney
Aeron D Peterson,	Graham Lentz	Maria Pia Karlsson	Peter & Sue Ellis
Alan Robbins	Hugh Brickell	Mark Baxter	Peter Jachimiak
Alan Wells	Ian 'Snowy' Snowball	Mark Davies	Phil Adamson
Amanda Lloyd	Ian McFarland	Mark Hynds	Philip Headford
Andrew Campbell	Ian Sheppard	Mark Jones	Rebecca Rodger
Andy *'Top Mod in Ponty'* Knowles	James Parker	Mark O'Flaherty	Robert Gillingham
Antony McCloskey	Jane Williams	Mark Rowley	Rod Gillan
Antony Shipman	Jason Brummell	Martyn Symour	Ross Perriman
Barry Bebbington	Jayne Thomas	Maurice Morgan	Russ Gallagher
Brian Coulson	John Kavanagh	Memo Torfilli	Sally Black
Carl Grisley	Julie Rug	Michael Caluan	Samantha Stevens
Chris Goosman	Karen Glaser	Michael Downes	Scott Riley
Chris Jones	Karen Jenkins	Michael Relguag	Sheenagh James
Clare Luton	Karen Maher	Michael W Salter	Sian Harvey
Clare Thrower	Kate Butler	Nick Pascoe	Simon Green
Dave English Anstee	Kerry Bennet	Nick Ward	Siobhan Nolan-Farmer
Dave Rimmer	Kevin Jones	Noreen Pearson	Stacey Blythe
Dave Williams	Lawrence Drew	Paul Boyce	Stephen Evans
Denise Allen	Lee Davies	Paul Hemmings	Stephen Mead
Douglas Friedli	Lee Flay	Paul Hooper-Keeley	Steve McColgan
Eddie Crole	Lee Jones	Paul (Mac) Macnamara	Tracy McNulty
Gabriela Giacoman	Lee Rees	Paul Mansfield	Tracey Williams
Gary Davies	Lesley Herbert	Paul Matthews	Victor Falsetta
Geoff Nicholas	Lolita Jones	Paul *'Sammy'* Thomas	Wynford Protheroe

There is one person who deserves a very special mention in this book because without him it would never have happened.

ALAN THOMPSON
BBC Radio Wales, presenter, producer, music lover
1963 – 2017

I was lucky enough to meet Alan Thompson when I was invited to go on his BBC Radio Wales Evening Show to record an item on Northern Soul. Al and I hit it off straight away. Both of us having got into mod as teenagers and being huge Jam fans. If Al was covering anything mod-related, I would get the call to come in and talk about it on air. Usually, however, we spent more time off-air chatting about music and the clothes etiquette of ageing mods.

Alan suggested we pitch a documentary idea about Welsh mods for TV and we worked on this over a period of about a year. We were unable to get it commissioned, so I pressed on with the idea of the book. Sadly Al passed away following a short illness on 28th September 2017. So he is not here to see the book come to life. He would have most certainly contributed to it.

Alan interviewed and met many famous people throughout his career – Paul McCartney, Ray Davies and of course Paul Weller. He'd drop the odd name, but it wasn't something he would brag about. However, it was this story that he told me on our way to London for the launch of Jam drummer, Rick Buckler's autobiography, that knocked the ball out of the proverbial park for me. So I thought it was worth repeating here.

Here it is as told in Al's inimitable style on his Facebook page.

"*28th November 1980, this little beauty was released…Sound Affects by The Jam. One afternoon in 1980, as a teenage mod, I blagged my way into the control room of Townhouse Studios in Shepherds Bush, London and sat with The Jam whilst they recorded the vocals to a song called Music For The Last Couple. Paul Weller let me have a go on his guitar (a red Gibson SG) and he made tea. The Jam smoked a lot, swore an AWFUL lot, and it was magnificent… I believe the modern term is… I SMASHED IT !!!*"

RIP Alan Thompson. Boy About Town

About the author

Claire is a journalist, editor and broadcaster with over 25 years experience in print and online media. She is also passionate about the mod scene. She is a regular contributor to modculture.com and writes a mod fashion blog for newuntouchables.com. She contributed the foreword to the first book on women in the mod scene – *Ready Steady Girls*, by Baxter, Brummell & Snowball. She has made regular appearances on BBC Radio Wales to speak about mod and 60s soul music and presented at the first Jam Literary Event in London. This is her first book.

About the photographer

Haydn has worked as a photographer for over twenty years. He has received numerous commissions along with British Council and Arts Council Awards to document communities and regions here in Wales and overseas. His photographs have figured in a number of exhibitions and publications and collections of his work are held at the National Library of Wales in Aberystwyth and Ffotogallery, Cardiff, Wales. Parallel with his photographic career, Haydn works as a documentary cameraman and director and won a BAFTA Cymru in 2000 and 2008.

Acknowledgements

Peter Jachimiak for his sterling social media support, Meurig Jones & the Mad Dog Scooter crew for a great few days in North Wales, Michael W Salter for his encouragement and help at the last hurdle, Jules Rees for putting me in touch with his father, Wyndham Rees, Mac, Eddie, Reevesy and Des Mannay for sharing their memorabilia and memories, Andrew Campbell for 'keeping the faith', my mum for always believing in me, my daughter Eira for just being her, Haydn for his incredible eye, Kevin for designing a book we can all be proud of and finally everyone who shared their memories and let us photograph them. *Diolch yn fawr iawn!*

Author: Claire Mahoney
Photography: Haydn Denman
Art direction: Kevin Bridgeman

Published in the United Kingdom by Dovetail Communications Ltd.

Printed in Wales by Gomer Press
www.gomerprinting.co.uk

British Library Cataloguing-in-Publication Data.
A CIP record for this book is available from the British Library.
ISBN: 978-1-5272-2051-5

Copyright © 2018 By Dovetail Communications Ltd
Photographs copyright © 2018 By Haydn Denman
www.haydndenman-photography.com

All photographs by Haydn Denman except where noted.

All rights reserved. No part of this publication may be reproduced, stored in a retrieval system or transmitted in any form or by any means; electronic, mechanical, photocopying, recording or otherwise, without prior permission of the publisher.

Every effort has been made to trace the copyright holders, but if any have been inadvertently overlooked the publishers will be pleased to make the necessary arrangements at the first opportunity.

All opinions expressed within this publication are those of the authors and not necessarily of the publisher.

welshmod.com

Dovetail Communications Ltd
4 Ynys Bridge Court, Gwaelod-Y-Garth, Cardiff,
United Kingdom, CF15 9SS

info@dovetailcomms.co.uk
www.dovetailcomms.co.uk